PLANET DAGENHAM

CHAMELEON

Jeremy Clarkson's

PLANET DAGENHAM

drivestyles **of the** rich **& famous**

First published in Great Britain in 1998 by

Chameleon Books

an imprint of

André Deutsch Ltd

76 Dean Street

London W1V 5HA

André Deutsch Ltd is a **VCI plc** company

www.vci.co.uk

Design: **Neal Townsend** @ **JMP Ltd**

Picture research: **Odile Schmitz** @ **JMP Ltd**

Printed by Butler & Tanner of Frome, Somerset and London

A catalogue record for this book is available from the British Library

ISBN 0 233-99335-5

For the children, Emily and Finlo, who stayed in the

playroom while I was writing this.

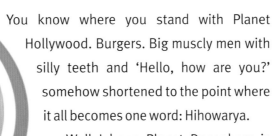

PLANET DAGENHAM

You know where you stand with Planet Hollywood. Burgers. Big muscly men with silly teeth and 'Hello, how are you?' somehow shortened to the point where it all becomes one word: Hihowarya.

Well I hope Planet Dagenham is similarly easy to understand. I could have called it 'Planet Liverpool' but people might have thought its central theme was the Beatles, or football. I could have called it Planet Coventry, but no one would have read it.

Dagenham says it all. Dagenham is small town Detroit and this is a small town car book which concerns itself not with the big picture, but the tiny little details.

There are four chapters: cars on film; cars in music and modelling; cars in television; and cars in sport, each of which took me ages to write.

Take it with you to the lavatory and while you're having a crap, have a laugh.

PLANET DAGENHAM

FILM

Ever since those rickety old days when people were sepia and walked quickly, the car has been a cinematic mainstay. Oh how they laughed when Buster Keaton's doors fell off. Just like they had done in his previous film. And the one before that. Then of course we had the car chase which today has become *de rigeur* in any action film. We must remember, though, that it isn't the chase which keeps the audiences queuing — it's the crash that ends it. Everyone likes a good car crash but it can be time-consuming standing at the side of the road waiting for one to happen and it's morally reprehensible to actually get out there and cause one. The cinema, therefore, is a pressure valve. And a useful marketing tool for the car industry, too. Where would Aston Martin be without James Bond? How many Mini Coopers would have been sold without *The Italian Job*? Would the Mustang have become an icon without *Bullitt*? And remember, until *Herbie* came along, the Beetle was a cheap and disgusting piece of Nazi memorabilia.

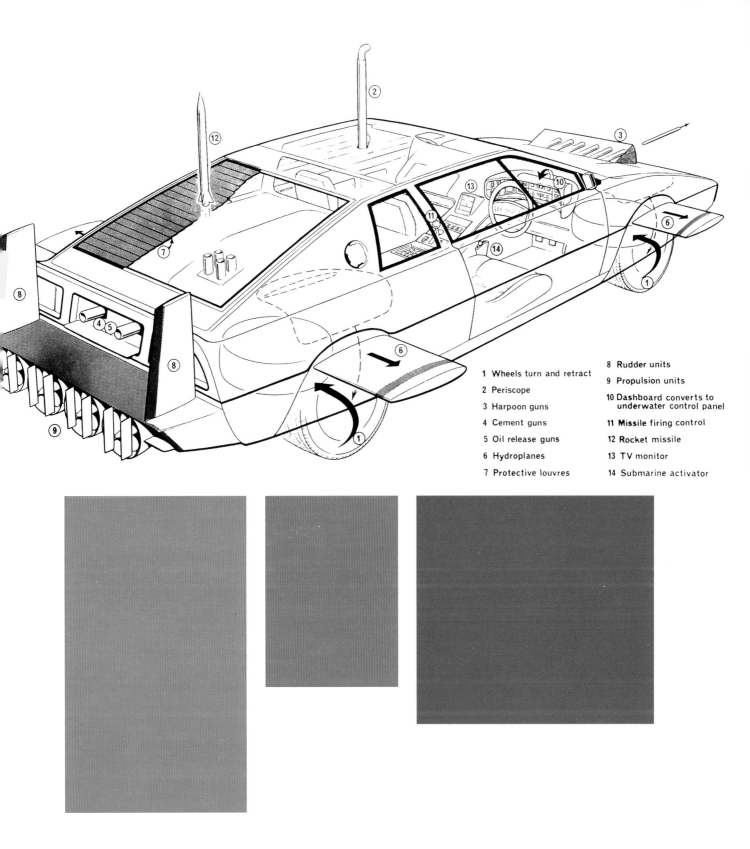

1 Wheels turn and retract
2 Periscope
3 Harpoon guns
4 Cement guns
5 Oil release guns
6 Hydroplanes
7 Protective louvres
8 Rudder units
9 Propulsion units
10 Dashboard converts to underwater control panel
11 **Missile** firing control
12 **Rocket** missile
13 TV monitor
14 Submarine activator

America vs Italy, V8 vs V12, Cobra vs Daytona. Evenly matched until the corners.

WHY ALL FILM CAR CHASES ARE WRONG

think it's fair to say that, after 25 years in prison, your driving skills would be a little rusty. You'd have been banged up when the world was driving around in Ford Cortinas and the M40 stopped at Oxford. You would be unfamiliar with speed humps, bus lanes and you'd be staggered by the sheer weight of traffic. Nevertheless, in *The Rock*, Sean Connery has been out of jail for just a couple of hours before he finds himself at the wheel of a Hummer, being chased by half of San Francisco's police force and an FBI agent in a Ferrari 355.

Does he get away? Does Dickie Davies take a photo of a badger to the hairdressers? He just comes out of prison, steals a car that he has never

★BIZARRE *1. Retired teacher John Anderson drove up to take his driving test… and ploughed through the exam*

The Ferrari 355. A very fast car. A very fast car indeed. A cop in a Ferrari leaves little hope for a con in a Hummer.

even seen before and out-manoeuvres anything that the forces of law and order care to throw his way... Well now ex-cuse-me, but even if we leave aside the oxidisation of Mr Connery's wheelmanship, there is another important issue here. The only place where a Hummer could get away from a Ferrari 355 is in the desert. In the streets of a major American city, he wouldn't even get 100 yards. It may have been a magnificent spectacle to watch this 3 ton truck driving through lorries with a yellow 355 Spider in hot pursuit but it took the very limits of credibility and shattered them. And it was much the same story in *Goldeneye*, Pierce Brosnan's first outing as Special Agent 007, Mr James Bond.

Over the years we have learned that that Mr Bond can out-drink and out-smoke any shark. We know that he never loses on the gaming tables of Monte Carlo and that he can identify fish at a hundred paces. Plus, he is more masculine than a powersliding Lamborghini Countach. However, even though I don't doubt for a second that he could out-drive Michael Schumacher, there is no way in hell that an Aston Martin DB5 could outrun a Ferrari 355, especially if the 355 in question is being driven by a Russian agent who, one presumes, can also out-shag a rabbit. A DB5 is for instance, propelled by a six cylinder 4 litre engine which produces 282 brake horsepower. The Ferrari has a 3.5 litre V8 which produces 380 bhp. The Ferrari is also lighter, better balanced and, thanks to a superior chassis and tyres, about 1,000 times faster through the corners.

In reality, the Russian agent would have reached Monaco, had a bath, got changed, hatched a plan to wreck the world and executed it while Bond was still wrestling with understeer on the first corner. Sure, Ferrari insisted that the 355 could not be seen to lose the encounter and so Bond gallantly

centre. John, 70, injured five people and caused £23,000 worth of damage when he smashed through a wall and ▶

Vanishing Point. What should be vanishing is the Challenger's gearbox.

waves the Russkie ahead. But they would never have been alongside in the first place. Ferrari always come a cropper in fantasy land.

Remember *Magnum*? Every week, Tom Selleck would drive around the island of Hawaii in his boss's 328 GTS failing to catch baddies in huge Yank tanks. Of course, he could have been in the wrong gear. This is one of life's abiding mysteries. In the same way that women fleeing for their lives always fall over, men in cars always drive along in third.

Take *Vanishing Point*, the 1971 cult classic that inspired Primal Scream's 1997 album of the same name. It's a fine film, if you're stoned, stuck in a 1960s time warp or a fan of happy-clappy gospel music. It's a fine film, too, if you like car chases, because you get little else. But the director Richard C. Sarafian should have been reminded with a crisp backhand slap that when your lead player is an ex-race car driver, he'd be in the right gear at the right time. But no. Our man Kowalski is thundering through the Nevada Desert in his supercharged Dodge Challenger when he is invited to race by another chap in a cut-down, souped-up E Type Jaguar.

The road is straight and I'm afraid therefore that the race is more pointless than a beach ball. A normal E Type would be able to do

careered into offices, wrecking desks and cabinets before coming to a halt under a sign saying 'Report Here for

145mph, whereas the racer we see should do considerably more. Now really, the very top speed of a standard Challenger is 113 mph. Even with the benefit of force-feeding from the super-charger, the wardrobe style aerodynamics would prevent it from doing much more than 130 mph. The Jag, then, would walk it.

But wait, what's this? The two cars are flat out and alongside when Kowalski

MY TOP 20 DRIVES

THE CAR	Ford Escort Cosworth Group A rally car.
THE PLACE	Ford's test track at Boreham, Essex.
THE DRIVER . . .	Gwyndaf Evans – who's bald, Welsh and mad.
THE MEMO	After one lap I felt rather sick. After two, I was.

changes down... and roars ahead! WHAAAT! Surely, in a film made *about* cars for people who *know and understand* cars, someone on set could have pointed out that you can't change down when you're flat out.

Well you can, but 16 small holes will appear in your bonnet as your valves free themselves from their mountings and go in search of extra-terrestrial life.

Have you seen *Days of Thunder*, the Tom Cruise vehicle film which sees him coming down from a world of hate in *Top Gun* to a world of tortured rubber as an American Nascar driver? It's not bad actually but, again, we are treated to a series of preposterous gearchanges. There is the diminutive Mr Cruise in the lead when someone attempts to come past. So what does Mr Cruise do? Why he changes down, of course. Sounds great. Looks idiotic. If you change from fifth to fourth in a Nascar racer at 200 mph, the engine will come flying into the car's cockpit via the air vents. You will then have to walk back to the pits, picking bits of camshaft out of your teeth, where Robert Duvall will hit you in the face with a wheel brace.

What I would like to do at this point is offer my services to any film-maker who feels his movie should feature a car chase. I will ensure the cars are evenly matched and that the drivers don't do anything silly. But don't worry, it'll still be exciting enough because the cars in question will be a Jaguar XJ220 and a McLaren F1. ⭐

Driving Test.' An embarrassed John, who had come to renew his licence after 42 years of crash-free motoring, ▶

Bond. Aston. Aston. Bond. Sherioushly shuited.

LICENSED TO THRILL – BOND ON FILM

James Bond, as we all know, changes his women like Blair changes his mind. But when it comes to serious matters such as cars, the man's fidelity is normally of Paul Newman and Joanne Woodward proportions: *Goldfinger*; *Thunderball*; *On Her Majesty's Secret Service*, all saw him at the wheel of Astons. And when he wasn't driving one it was either because he was abroad or on top of a broad.

But then, lo and behold, in *The Spy Who Loved Me*, Q pops off the

claimed his accelerator had jammed. Officials at the Los Angeles driving centre said he could take it another day,

Sardinian ferry at the wheel of a Lotus Esprit and the Aston is left thrashing about in the piranha tank. So what went wrong? How did Norfolk stick the poison shoe into Newport Pagnell?

In truth it was a move 007 himself would have been proud of. On one ordinary cold British day, Don McLauchlan, the Public Relations boss at Lotus, went to visit a friend who worked at Pinewood studios. Like any British sports car executive, he would have given his marriage implements to poach Bond from Aston Martin, and when his friend told him *The Spy Who Loved Me* was in the middle of shooting, he decided to seize the day.

'The new Esprit wasn't even ready,' says Don, 'but I rushed back and hurried them into finishing off a prototype version, then returned to see my friend at Pinewood.'

Don parked the car outside the Bond offices, then sat with his friend and waited for the production crew to break for lunch. Naturally, when they came out, they formed a big crowd around the strange new Lotus. The next bit, for Don, was the biggest gamble of all: 'I really wanted to create some mystique against the Aston,' says Don. 'So I walked out and, instead of talking to the Bond people, forced myself to ignore them and just push through the crowd and drive off.' Don was hoping the Bond people would make the effort to find him, and sure enough big Bond boss Cubby Broccoli rang Lotus the next day.

Spool forward to Sardinia and the filming of the mountain chase and underwater sequence. It's early morning and Don is up with the larks, or whatever the Sardinian equivalent is, washing the Lotus before filming starts. His hand goes for the bucket, but a second hand gets there first and grabs the spare chamois. A voice says: 'Good morning, would you like some help cleaning the car?' The name was Moore... Roger Moore.

THE FILMS

There have been 18 Bond films, providing you don't count the misguided flop that was *Never Say Never Again* or the precursor to it all – *Casino Royale,* which had David Niven cast, rather incongruously, as the hero. Now, in that time, Bond has been everywhere and slept with everyone up to and probably including Major Boothroyd – a.k.a. Q. He knows everything and has driven, flown and sailed pretty much every type of vehicle. There have been a great many cars, too, but despite the best efforts of BMW we

If he'd had the Z3, Bond would still be in the shed.

all know that the great man drives an Aston Martin DB5. Aficionados of the books will tell you that he actually has a Bentley, and for sure we see the car in question in *From Russia With Love*. But it was in *Goldfinger*, the first of the true 007 blockbusters, that we were first introduced to that modified Aston.

At the time, Aston were a well-known force in the world of motor racing but in Botswana, frankly, no one had ever heard of them. It was a call from a Bond producer to the company's HQ in Newport Pagnell that changed everything. All over the world, Aston Martin is James Bond.

The government car issued to 007 for his one man war with organised crime was the 4 litre DB5 – gentlemanly, elegant and, with a top speed of 140 mph, powerful, too. He used it again in *Thunderball* and remained loyal to the brand on his wedding day when he and Diana Rigg set off for their honeymoon in a DBS. It was a puny six-cylinder version, incidentally, but wore V8 badges and was subjected to a V8 soundtrack to hammer the message home. It could even squeal its tyres on sand.

By this stage, though, film-makers were starting to realise that companies with a little more financial clout than Aston could be used to help market the films and so the links with Aston were severed. And they

LOTUS: Loads Of Trouble, Usually Serious.

stayed broken until 1987, when Timothy Dalton took over for *The Living Daylights*. Three Vantages were supplied to the film-makers for the chase sequence, which saw Bond evading the entire Czechoslovakian army, and a V8 Volante was used for sequences in England.

Several years later, while wandering around the Pinewood Studios, where the *Goldfinger* chase sequence was filmed and where all the Bond films until *Goldeneye* were made, I found those Vantages, stacked on top of each other in a shed. Cry? I wept buckets. And then I wept some more when news trickled out that BMW had waved a big cheque under M's nose and, as a result, had been given permission to provide the cars for *Goldeneye*. Bond in a BMW. It was a ridiculous notion. And obviously the film-makers realised this because at the beginning of the film we saw him back where he belongs, in the DB5, racing a Ferrari 355, winning and at the same time charming a girl out of her knickers. The only time he ever actually used the Z3 was to dry his hair. But then, as we know, that's all the Z3 is good for.

Here's the question though. Are there any cars that Bond has driven over the years which really would make a better companion today than the great DB5?

Bond checks his look in the mirror, only to find that he's being followed by a hearse. The chase, naturally, is on…

DR NO – SUNBEAM ALPINE

Had it been the Tiger version with the 4.7 litre V8, then maybe, but the Alpine with its engine lifted out of a toaster was not fast enough, noisy enough or cool enough. Nice in its time but today – way past its prime. Of course, had he used the Tiger it would have been Bond and not the pursuing villains in their hearse that went over the ravine. And this would have spoiled the film somewhat. And rather curtailed the opportunity for a follow up.

FROM RUSSIA WITH LOVE – BENTLEY

In a bid to stay faithful to the original Ian Fleming books, Bond was seen to be driving a Bentley, but while there is a strong argument for putting him in the Arnage today, I'm not sure the intervening models would have been suitable. They're too big, and they don't go round corners fast enough. It would have been really rather embarrassing if the Czech army using Ladas had caught Bond's Mulsanne. And I suspect they would have.

★BIZARRE *2. While on patrol in South London, policeman Richard Pooley came across an illegally parked Saab*

YOU ONLY LIVE TWICE – TOYOTA 2000GT

Obviously, with the film set in Japan, Bond had to use a Japanese car, which today would have been easy. They would have given him a Skyline GTR and that would have been that. But remember, we're talking here about 1967 – just 22 years after two major Japanese cities were flattened by atom bombs. The Japanese car industry had been eased off the ground with help – can you believe it – from Austin, but it was still in the nest, sitting there with its beak open. Bond needed a sports car though and that meant it was either a Honda S600, which was too weedy, or a Toyota 2000GT which had exactly the same sort of chassis as a Lotus Elan, all independent suspension, rack and pinion steering and magnesium alloy wheels.

It was, therefore, advanced and with a 2.3 litre straight six and a five speed manual gearbox it was pretty nippy, too. Top speed was 135 mph. However, at nearly $7,000 dollars it was pricier than either the new Porsche 911 or the E Type Jaguar. And it was a coupe – not a convertible – something that the producers had specifically requested. Toyota, however, made two special soft tops for Bond and how did he repay them? By coming home and never driving the 2000GT again. Mind you, who can blame him? He had a DB5, remember.

and wrote out a ticket for it. PC Pooley then slapped the ticket firmly on the windscreen and watched in horror as ▶

DIAMONDS ARE FOREVER –
FORD MUSTANG MACH ONE

Bond first experienced a Mustang in *Thunderball*, where he could be seen glancing at the speedo and wondering how, when it said 100 mph, they appeared to be going at 500 mph. Oh the joys of speeded-up film. Of course, for the epic Las Vegas chase, it wasn't the classic '65 but one of the last of the great pony cars. Called the Mach One, it had a 350 cubic inch V8 which developed 330 bhp and was therefore an enormously powerful and enormous car which could do 0-60 in 6.5 seconds.

It was the biggest Mustang ever made and as the Vegas police force found out, it was also just about the fastest... and the cleverest. In the chase it goes into the narrow alley on its two left-hand wheels and comes out at the other end on its two right-hand wheels. Clever stuff, but soon afterwards the oil crisis hit and the Mustang was emasculated by a muffled 2.3 litre four cylinder motor. Sad, but that's not the issue here. The issue is this: would Bond have been better off today with a Mach One Mustang than with a DB5?

To which the answer is a resounding no. A Mustang may be alright for a maverick New York policeman with an errant wife and a drink problem, but Bond is a Commander in the Royal Navy and you can't turn up for dinner in Whitehall in the motorised equivalent of a cheeseburger.

THE MAN WITH THE GOLDEN GUN –
AMC HORNET

Yes indeed, the Torville and Dean leap with rotation stunt was very clever and the performance from Sheriff JW Pepper made audiences around the world laugh. But AMC made joke cars and the Hornet used by Bond was the punch line. He was, of course, chasing a Matador Brougham which turned itself into a plane, but then 007's Hornet wasn't exactly standard either. It had toughened suspension, a six-cylinder engine, a centred steering wheel and a special fuel system to stop the car from stalling as it turned over.

THE SPY WHO LOVED ME –
LOTUS ESPRIT

And into the breech stepped Lotus who provided Bond with the first incarnation of its Guigaro-designed, 2.2 litre, four-cylinder, mid-engined

the car rolled off backwards down the hill, only coming to a halt when it smashed into a brick wall. The car's owner,

Not Bond's first choice. The 2CV – a lawnmower with a roof.

Esprit supercar. There's more. In the film, it could go underwater, drop mines and shoot helicopters from the sky with its surface-to-air missiles. Wow. But at this stage of Bond's career, diehard fans – and I count myself among their number – were becoming just a little bit irritated with the jokey direction our hero was taking. And the Esprit seemed to typify this. It was fun, but unlike the Aston it wouldn't hit you in the face with a hammer.

FOR YOUR EYES ONLY – CITROËN 2CV

After the debacle that was *Moonraker*, the script-writers brought Bond back to earth with a simple Brits v the Russkies yarn. But while the essence was back, the Aston wasn't. Bond started out with a white Esprit which, thankfully, was blown to kingdom come, but they then replaced it with a bronze turbo, which as far as I know is still parked outside a bar in Cortina – very appropriate.

This film, however, was memorable mainly for Bond's first ever outing in a Citroën 2CV. Needless to say, he was immediately familiar with the layout of the gearbox and managed to outrun the baddies who came at him in a selection of Peugeot 504s. Most ended up in trees or spinning around on their roofs in a hilarious fashion. Bond meanwhile kept the 2CV in one piece even though it too had been upside down and back to front and rolled down a hillside. I really can't imagine why anyone would want to go back to the DB5 after this.

a garage mechanic, not only had to pay for the body repair because his hand brake was faulty, but was also forced ▶

Alfa Romeo GTV6 – in which Bond races to stop a nuclear explosion. Good job it had just been serviced.

OCTOPUSSY – ALFA ROMEO GTV6

Here's what happened. Desperate to save the world from a nuclear holocaust, Bond leapt into an Alfa Romeo GTV6 and, right under the nose of the German police force, used it to reach the bomb just in time. Phew. But here's what would have happened in reality. Desperate to save the world from a nuclear holocaust, Bond would have seen the GTV6 and clocked it, rightly, for a sporty Italian coupe with enough punch to get him to the bomb on time. So he would have leapt inside only to find that if he put the seat in the right position for his legs, he wouldn't have been able to reach the wheel. Moving it forwards would have put his knees behind his ears. And all the while, air would have been escaping from the tyres. But hey, this wouldn't have mattered because it wouldn't have started anyway, and even if it had, the gear linkage would have disintegrated.

But let's just say that had he got it going, he wouldn't have gone very far before all the electrics packed up. Mind you, this would have been a good thing because come the first corner, he'd have been unable to move the wheel – partly because he could never have reached it and partly because there was no power assistance for the steering.

I know all this because I used to have a GTV6 and I therefore know he'd have arrived to diffuse the bomb, on foot, about 25 minutes after it had gone off. He'd have been reduced to his component parts, Russia would have invaded Western Europe, we'd all be Commies now and the world would never have heard of Tony Blair. Damn. Why did you have to make it on time James? Just for once, you could have been late. But I do understand why you never drove an Alfa again. When you're in the business of saving the world, you need reliability above all else. A Corolla, perhaps. Or a DB5.

to stump up for the parking ticket. ★BIZARRE★

Right, I'm going back to *The Persuaders.*

A VIEW TO A KILL – RENAULT 11

This one may have featured the best looking of all the Bond babes – Tanya Roberts – and for sure it had the best baddie, in the shape of Christopher Walken. But car-wise, it was something of a low point. In a bid to save California from becoming a giant swimming pool, Bond was forced to tear through Paris in a Renault 11. But fortunately for us, Paris did the decent thing and tore through the Renault 11. The roof was sliced off by a barrier and then, in another collision, the rear end was removed. In his Aston that would have been 'game over', but the front drive layout meant Bond could keep going and California was allowed to carry on imposing no smoking rules in bars and cafes.

LICENCE TO KILL – A LORRY

After a brief trip round Florida in a rented Lincoln Mark VIII, Bond's only high speed action came at the wheel of a Kenworth truck. Bond, lorry. Lorry, Bond. The words, I'm afraid, don't sit together terribly comfortably.

GOLDENEYE – ASTON MARTIN DB5

Bond gets his Aston back. And long may he stay in it.

We have lift off. The baddies' Dodge Charger passes that Beetle – again.

BULLITT (POSITIVELY THE BEST FILM WITH CARS IN IT, EVER)

Let's be honest here: San Francisco is one of the world's most stupid cities. First of all, it is ridiculously hilly, so walking is not really an option. And even the strongest, most powerfully-flanked horse would have struggled in those early days to get from the harbour up to Nob Hill. This is bad enough, but to make things worse, it's built right on top of one of the world's most vigorous and exciting geological faults — the San Andreas.

This means that once every so often, the earth moves in such a way that all the buildings fall over. I'm sure the early gold prospectors who founded this city by the bay didn't realise this at the time but after the earthquake of 1906, no one was in any doubt. Now what they should have done at this point is give up — the gold was running out anyway —

but instead, they rebuilt it and even allowed it to expand still further.

You see, by this time, the car and the cinema had been invented and the city fathers knew that, one day, their remarkable and unique urban scrawl would be able to bring the two together in the most spectacular fashion possible. It happened in 1968 when Peter Yates made *Bullitt*.

Now I know that during the 9 minute 42 second centrepiece car chase, they went past the same VW Beetle six times and I also know that we see the same Pontiac Firebird more than once, too. But this is forgivable. It would even have been forgivable if, halfway though, Steve McQueen had turned to the camera and said 'I'm gay, you know.' This, you see, is the finest car chase ever.

First of all, there was no music, unless, that is, you count the aural bombardment of those two colossal V8s. And then there was the performance from McQueen, who really did a fine line in determined concentration. It's hard to look like you have problems with your love life, a corrupt boss and an entanglement with the mafia when you aren't allowed to speak, or pull faces. Bill Hickman, as the driver of the Charger, was good, too, especially as he was more stuntman than actor. When he put his seat belt on, you knew you were dealing with someone who wouldn't spin out at the first corner and change down all the time.

And then there was San Francisco. They used Taylor Street predominantly because the jumps are that much more dramatic, and come on, can you think of anywhere that would look better? Bruges? Padstow? I think not. San Francisco was built for one reason and one reason alone — to be the car chase capital of the world. But strangely, the success of the *Bullitt* chase had nothing to do with the location, or the acting or the plot. It was simple. Here were two big American muscle cars being driven the way we'd all like to drive them.

Petrolheads everywhere would saw off their own feet for a chance to dice in real live traffic for death or glory. The only thing that could possibly be more fun than racing a Dodge Charger through San Francisco is watching Robin Cook's trousers fall down. I'd love to see what he has in his pants. It must be huge, the penile equivalent of a V8.

But the big question is this. Given that both drivers were equal, which of those two American muscle cars would, in real life, have been able to outpace the other.

THE BAD GUYS' DODGE CHARGER

The Dodge wades into this contest with one inner city problem — it is vast. Driving this in a confined street really is like trying to thread a camel through the eye of a needle — it can be done but only if, first of all, you pass it through a food blender.

To put some figures on it, the Charger is more than 17 feet long which means that if two were parked end to end, you could use them as a bridge to the Moon. This car is even longer than the Jaguar XJ220. Long is too small a word. It is verylongindeed. However, the distance between its wheels is not long at all. The Charger has the wheelbase of a small Japanese supermini, which means were are talking here about overhangs of a type that could guarantee it a slot in *Baywatch*.

It's been worked out, by me actually, that 14 people could live and work under the front overhang of a Dodge Charger and 12 at the back. So already we can guess that this car is not set up for corners. And we're right. The suspension is not made up of coils and dampers, as you might expect, but of RSJs and yoghurt. It's an interesting idea but it doesn't work terribly well. And nor does the steering. It is power assisted, of course, but to go from lock to lock, you need to turn the wheel five times. In other words, before attempting to apply some opposite lock, you really needed to attach the centre hub to a high-powered drill.

But you'd better be alert in case you need to stop. The Charger, you see, was supplied with drum brakes all round. Despite the weight, and the size, discs were an option! Small wonder then that in the film, the baddies made for open country where the road straightens out. In this kind of environment, they could unleash the Charger's most potent weapon — its R/T *Rapid Transit* motor — a 7.2 litre V8 which churned out 375 bhp — the same as a Ferrari 355 — and a massive 480 ft/lbs of torque — the same as an oil tanker. They must have reckoned that Mr McQueen's Mustang would be lost in the haze of their petrol fumes.

However, even though the Charger's headlamps were hidden behind vacuum-propelled covers for better aerodynamics, we're still talking here about something that cleaves the air with the efficiency of a fat boy. So the top speed was just 127 mph. In the lower speed ranges, though, where aerodynamics matter less, the Dodge was amazing. With a four speed manual box, it could haul itself in a cloud of tyre smoke from 0-60 in just

★BIZARRE *3. Dancer Belinda Fraine is possibly the only woman in the world to have caused a multiple pile-up*

6.5 seconds. It really was something of a thunderstorm this car — loud, dark and capable of moving around — randomly — at great speed. It was the chaos theory made real.

STEVE MCQUEEN'S FORD MUSTANG

McQueen's Ford, in a straight line, should be no match for the Charger. In fact, I'm surprised it moved at all with such a puny engine.

Yes, it was a V8 but it only displaced 6.4 litres which in a world where fuel was just 10 cents a gallon made it something of an economy car. Shall I buy a Mini, or a Mustang? Oh what the hell, I'll have the Ford — it's prettier. It was pretty, too. No wait, what am I talking about here? It still is pretty in a *Xena, Warrior Princess* sort of way. It had big haunches aft of the doors, mildly flared arches and wonderful blacked-out wheels, but this was just jewellery on what is still an all-time classic shape.

However, the big plus point was this: the Mustang was a compact. Because it was only 15 feet long, and because it weighed two hundredweight less than the Charger, it didn't need so much grunt. It didn't have it, either. The miserable 6.4 litre V8 churned out just 325 bhp, and only 427 ft/lbs of torque. But thanks to the Angel Delight body, it could hit 125 mph. And guess what, from 0-60, it took 6.5 seconds as well. These cars really were evenly matched.

In a battle through the corners, though, the Ford would win. It had a limited slip differential and anti tramp bars to stop the rear axle leaping from county to county in full bore, pedal to the metal take-offs.

The steering was better too. There was no power assistance so driving at slow speeds it was easy to

MY TOP 20 DRIVES	
THE CAR	Lamborghini Diablo VT.
THE PLACE	Bruntingthorpe Proving Ground, Leicestershire.
THE DRIVER . . .	Chief Lambo test driver, Valentino 'Bloody' Bilbao.
THE MEMORY . .	It was the first time I'd ever done a 360 degree spin, followed by another 360 degree spin at 150 mph.

with her breasts. Miss Fraine, from Melbourne, Australia, went out and got smashed after winning £100,000 on ▶

see where the term 'muscle car' came from, but once you were moving it became quite direct. There's no way that, through town, the Charger could have gotten away. And it didn't, of course. Contemporary experts and those who drive the cars today all agree that the Mustang was faster through the turns and a damn sight easier to drive hard and fast. Out of town, Dodge fans say the Charger was faster — but only just — while other suggest it would have been a close run thing.

I've driven both cars, though, and would close by saying this: Unless you were really, really good behind the wheel, you'd end up crashing the Dodge into a couple of walls, and then a petrol station where you would be burned to death. Which, strangely in the work of fiction that was *Bullitt*, is exactly what happened...

HOW THE CAR CHASE WAS FILMED

It took 1,000 years to build the Roman Empire, but just two weeks to shoot the rather more interesting car chase in *Bullitt*. However, before any fender bending began, the film crew had to decide what style of chase to make, and on this point McQueen called the shots. The star was determined to avoid any Hollywood special effects nonsense, instead going for the 'less is more' approach. He simply wanted the cars to be noisy and hit things. McQueen's desire to get the chase right was a major reason why he called in Englishman Peter Yates to direct the film, having admired the way Yates handled the gritty chase sequences in the gritty crime thriller *Robbery*, starring the equally gritty Stanley Baker.

'The realism was what made Bullitt so great,' says crew member Bud Ekins. 'Steve was determined not to pull any tricks like altering the speed of the film to make the cars look like they were going faster. He reckoned if we did it right we'd get the excitement out of the natural speed of the cars, so we ended up doing about 70 mph on the city streets and 100 mph-plus on the open road.'

At least that's what I think he said. It's hard to be sure because I conducted most of these conversations with Mr Ekins on my knees, tongue lapping at the edges of his shoes; as would you, because this is the man who actually drove the Mustang. Originally, McQueen was going to do all his own driving and Bud, as one of Steve's biking buddies, had been hired merely to stunt drive one of the background cars. 'But early

the lottery, and by night-time was so drunk she decided to stand in the middle of the highway and strip naked. A

Steve 'Le Mans' McQueen – apparently cool, but as tense as a Puma.

on in the shooting,' recalls Bud, 'Steve overcooked it on the corner and spun out, nearly hitting a cameraman. The scene stayed in the film, but the stunt co-ordinator, Carey Loftin, shouted to get Steve away from his car and the next thing I was having my hair dyed blonde. Don't get me wrong. Steve was a brilliant driver, but he always thought he could drive better than he could. If there was a rock in the middle of a desert, he'd hit it.'

The Dodge Charger, the villains' car, was driven by Hollywood stunt legend Bill Hickman, a man Bud remembers fondly as 'a complete drunk — I knew he had a hangover when we were doing the filming in the morning.' Nevertheless, the two principal stunt drivers worked well together, with even the famous jumping sequence being shot in one take. 'Actually, filming that part was the only bit that made me nervous,' says Bud. 'I was chasing Hickman and I knew he would do it flat out, just chewing up the cars every time they hit the ground, whereas I wanted to do it throttle on, throttle off as we rode the bumps — that way the cars would have sailed instead of bouncing and it would have looked just as good, but I had to follow his lead to keep up. The cars survived but we bent the flywheel on the Mustang, which a Ford engineer will tell you is impossible.'

Hickman's beer-guided driving wasn't the only problem with the hill sequence; McQueen was itching to get back in the car and drive this part himself: 'So what we did was tell Steve he could do it, and to turn up for

passing trucker slammed on his brakes to get a better look and caused a pile-up involving seven other vehicles. ▶

shooting at 10.00 am,' says Bud. 'But we actually tricked him and started three hours earlier. When he arrived and saw what was going on, he comes at me yelling "You sonofabitch, you did it to me again. I had to go on TV and tell everyone I didn't do the jump in *Great Escape* (Bud had done that too) and now this." But all the time he had a smile on his face. The guy was a complete professional at the end of the day.'

McQueen did get to do one nifty bit of driving, in the part where the Mustang swerves to avoid the motorcyclist who's fallen off his bike. For this stunt Bud played the biker while McQueen took the wheel of the Ford.

To make the most of the paltry number of streets closed off for them by the city authorities, the film crew shot most of the action from different angles simultaneously, using four cameras and then edited the best bits together. This is why the Dodge Charger loses six hubcaps and the famous green Beetle gets overtaken six times — you're seeing the same shot from different viewpoints. The tracking was done from a specially stripped down Corvette — still in use on *The Blues Brothers* many years later — and in addition several cameras were locked at fixed points along the chase. 'There's one shot where the Dodge crashes into a car and smashes up a camera — that wasn't bad driving. Bill was told to deliberately destroy it,' remembers Bud. 'Steve knew it would look good and just took the chance that the film would be usable.'

The wear and tear of the chase also ate up two Fords and three Dodges, all of them prepared by Steve's mechanic friend Max Balchowsky. Max chose, as Frank Bullitt's car, the 325 bhp 390Gt Mustang because, being a high performance version, he recalls 'it would cost the studio the least amount in labour and parts to prep it for the chase.' Apparently, Hollywood had something called budgets back then. In the end, Balchowsky did very little tuning to any of the engines, concentrating instead on stiffening the springs and fitting Koni shock absorbers to the Mustang. The Charger, he remembers, with 50 extra horsepower and 50 odd more lbs of torque, would leave the Mustang for dead, but the Ford was much tighter through the corners.

The greatest chase of all time was also responsible for one of the biggest cinematic cock-ups since Roger Moore was given an Equity card. At the climax, the ne'er-do-wells in the Dodge career off into the inferno of an exploding petrol station. Look closely, though, and you'll see on film the

Dodge trundling merrily off behind the erupting fuel pumps. In fact the stunt co-ordinator had released the cable holding the Dodge at the wrong moment, but before the director had time to say 'er...' the petrol station was already settling over ten states.

What also makes the *Bullitt* chase so uniquely knee-trembling, besides the driving, is the sound of those monstrous V8s shattering your telly speakers — the only time something from America has ever been worth listening to. Again, Bud recalls another tasty tale on this subject: 'Steve was determined not to put any soundtrack music over the chase and just leave it all to the engines. But when they'd edited it together he got cold feet and called in Quincy Jones, of all people, and asked him for a second opinion. So this big music guy watches the chase, and at the end he turns to McQueen and says: "That don't need no mother****** music."'

The engine sounds were recorded after filming, with Bud driving both cars round the race track at Willow Springs while the sound man sat next to him: 'He recorded some stuff with the windows a quarter of the way open, then half way, then three quarters and so on,' says Bud. 'There are two things I never worked out,' he adds. 'The first is why the soundman did that with the windows.' And the second? 'What the film is about.' ★

Gone In Sixty Seconds. Winner of longest car chase Oscar. Runner-up in best parking.

THE CAR CHASE OSCARS

The Gaumont in Dagenham has never seen anything quite like it. At exactly 6 pm the first limousine slides up to the kerb: it's a Hyundai Stellar finished in shimmering beige and from the back seat creaks Reg Crikey and his magnificent wife, Mrs Crikey. Soon, the High Street — bathed in late summer drizzle — is echoing to the sounds of blaring car horns as Nissan after Nissan disgorges people in glittering anoraks for the gala evening. Over there, Kevin Morley in a C&A bomber jacket. And coming up now is Peter Kinnaird in a Rover rally jacket, on loan for the evening from Millets. There is a sea of all the top names — Freeman, Hardy, Willis, Harry and even Fenton — the list goes on and on.

It is Oscar night... with a difference. It is the night when, for the first time, car enthusiasts are brought together to honour the finest car chases in cinema history. Presiding is Tiff Needell, who will do almost anything for a free supper.

Sense And Sensibility – 2 horsepower, racing wheels, idiotic outfits.

SHORTEST CAR CHASE

And the nominations are: *Sense And Sensibility, Braveheart, Das Boot, The Railway Children*

★ And the winner is – *Das Boot*, which could have had a car chase in it, but didn't.

LONGEST CAR CHASE

The nominations are: *The Blues Brothers, Gone In 60 Seconds, The Cannonball Run, The Italian Job*

★ And the winner is – *Gone In 60 Seconds*. The plot-line is over pretty much before the credits have stopped rolling. A gang of car thieves need a Mach One Mustang to complete a shipment of stolen cars but it gets horribly smashed up in the 90 minute chase that ensues.

BEST CAR CHASE

The nominations are: *The Italian Job, Bullitt, The French Connection, Vanishing Point*

★ And the winner is – *Bullitt,* which pitches into battle two equally talented drivers and two perfectly matched cars. There's no music and a big bang at the end.

Congratulations Mr Cruise, you win our award for pointless downchanging. Sorry, *Dukes Of Hazzard* won the award for best use of a window.

WORST EXAMPLE OF POINTLESS DOWNCHANGING

And the nominations are: Barry Newman in *Vanishing Point,* Tom Cruise in *Days Of Thunder,* Ken Berry in *Herbie Rides Again*

★ And the winner is – Tom Cruise (and while you're there Tom, could you tell us how, exactly, you got such a dirty face while racing?)

STUPIDEST CAR CHASE

And the nominations are: John Travolta and Nicolas Cage in *Face/Off,* David Caruso and baddies in *Jade,* Sean Connery and Nicolas Cage in *The Rock*

★ And the winners are – Sean Connery and Nicolas Cage for *The Rock*. Nic wins his for being such a terrible driver, while Sean gets his for being such a good one (imagine, a Ferrari 355 being incapable of catching a Hummer!).

MY TOP 20 DRIVES

THE CAR. . . . . . Toyota Starlet.
THE PLACE . . . . Portugal.
THE DRIVER . . . Me.
THE MEMORY . . It was one of the first press launches I'd ever been on and I simply couldn't believe a major, multi-national company would fly me all the way to Portugal, put me up in the best hotel and then let me play with one of their cars. But they did, and I went mad. It may have only had a one litre engine, but that car flew.

MOST CARS DESTROYED

And the nominations are: *The Blues Brothers, The Italian Job, Caddyshack*
★ And the winner is – *The Blues Brothers*; over 2,000 vehicles destroyed.

LEAST CONVINCING CATACLYSMIC ENDING

And the nominations are: *Vanishing Point, Thelma And Louise, Girl On A Motorcycle, Two Lane Blacktop*
★ And the winner is – *Vanishing Point*. Did that Challenger hit the bloody bulldozers? Or didn't it?

Norman Wisdom… sorr[
George Lazenby as Bon[
in *On Her Majesty's
Secret Service,* with
Diana Rigg as, yes,
Mrs Bond, in the last
sighting of the Aston
Martin for some time.

MOST IMPROBABLE SOUND EFFECTS
And the nominations are: *On Her Majesty's Secret Service,
Herbie Rides Again, The Cars That Ate Paris, Mad Max (I-III)*
★ And the winner is – *On Her Majesty's Secret Service*, where in his first,
and last, outing as 007, George Lazenby climbs into a Aston Martin DBS
which is parked on a sandy beach. As he sets off we hear the tyres squeal.
George was sacked for this and Sean came back in a wig.

BEST VEHICULAR MATCH
And the nominations are: *Bullitt, The Italian Job, Two Lane Blacktop,
French Connection*
★ And the winner is – *Bullitt*. Of course.

FUNNIEST VEHICULAR MISMATCH
And the nominations are: *The Rock, What's Up, Doc?, Duel, Goldeneye*
★ And the winner is – *What's Up, Doc?* Barbra Streisand pedals a pizza
delivery boy's bike up and down the streets of San Francisco with Ryan
O'Neal seated on the front. They are chased by three very large American
cars. Babs and Ryan then get into a Beetle. And are never caught. ★

WELCOME TO HOLLYWOOD

THE LINCOLN CONTINENTAL

Once upon a time, the average American believed that their enormous, sprawling country was in fact, the entire world. Travel west of Los Angeles or east of New York, and you'd fall into space. Hollywood, of course, was to blame. Hollywood told its audiences that beyond America 'there be witches'. But since American crews and studios became a tad expensive and other countries started offering facilities for 30p, producers have been making more and more films outside the mighty US of A: *Mission Impossible*; *Braveheart*; *Full Metal Jacket*; and so on.

That's why so many of America's current acting superstars are driving around in Range Rovers. They've been over here, seen this rather elegant sport utility vehicle and taken one home as a sort of souvenir. Nice. But, of course, in the days when they never went further than LA, they didn't know about England or Germany. So they bought American cars. And customised them. Oh dear.

Now, you might assume, as I did, that a mightily winged Cadillac would have been the car of choice for those who lived behind electronic gates in Beverly Hills. But, in fact, they all seemed to prefer the rather more restrained, though equally daft and pointless, Lincoln Continental. Tony Curtis may have used a Ferrari Dino in *The Persuaders* but back at home he reverted to type and had not one but two Lincolns, one of which dated back to 1941. It seems both it and he were to have featured in a film called *The Bugsy Seigel Story*, but after the project was canned, the two stayed together. Only he made some changes. This involved stripping the car back to bare metal and painting it in maroon with 25 coats of nitro cellulose lacquer. Not bad so far but then he added white wall tyres, burgundy carpets and seats trimmed in avocado green vinyl. Poor, Tony. Very poor. Robert Vaughan also had a Continental and, not to be outdone by Curtis, chose to have this 1962 four-door convertible altered so that the spare wheel was housed in a remoulded rear bumper. Inside, he fitted wood trim, a television and an eight-track sound system.

Now, I want to make it plain that not all actors of the era lost their automotive marbles. Both David Carradine and Ursula Andress had tasty BMW 507s, while Clint was a devotee of the prancing horse. But then Jayne Mansfield had a 1956, Mark Two Continental which cost her a massive $35,000. The special, and rather sudden, pearl paint was imported from the Orient. Wherever the hell that is. The entire interior was trimmed in mink but rather cleverly, this could be removed to prevent people from stealing it. Or, more likely, vomiting on it.

In the world of music, Glen Campbell had a Conti which was remarkably standard – apart, that is, from a white padded landau top with chrome hand-formed landau irons. Barry White went further. He had the whole car finished in white. And I do mean everything. Still it could have been worse. Singer Mel Tormé (no, I haven't heard of him either) is said to have been more fond of older British cars – a man of taste then. Er, no. It seems that his E Type was fitted with orange seats.

DA-NA NA-NA NA-NA NA-NA – BATMOBILE

Hollywood has tried many times to make a Batmobile but none has quite matched the sheer, jaw-snapping impact of the very first. It had such an effect on every small boy in the world that, even today, any car which looks slightly wacky gets the Bat tag. Even BMW, known for their strict and

★BIZARRE *4. A circus lorry travelling through Mexico crashed when its brakes failed on a bend. Unfortunately,*

regimented policy of giving cars numbers, not names, are happy to refer to the be-winged, racing 3.2 CSL as 'The Batmobile'.

Created for the TV series by veteran Californian customiser, George Barris, the original Batmobile was based on a 1957 concept car — the Lincoln Futura. This was a great idea but when you're making a weekly show, it's no good having just one car. You need several for close-up shots, promotional activities and, budget permitting, for the second unit to work on. Problem. There was only one Lincoln Futura so Barris had to base the subsequent models on stretched Fords. They worked, too, and one, used during the high-speed sequences, was even equipped with fully-fledged slick tyres at $1,000 dollars a go. The braking 'chutes were also fully functional, as Barris proved when he tested them on a normal highway, not knowing he was being observed at the time by two Highway Patrol policemen. He told them he was making

Holy pollution, Robin. Look at the size of this motor!

sure the car was right 'so that Batman and Robin can help you guys catch the Riddler'. And they let him off. However, the Batmobile was not an easy car to drive. The bubble windscreen distorted everything that wasn't dead ahead, it overheated constantly, and the steering broke with a regular monotony. And more disappointments. The engine wasn't really atomic and the flames we saw coming out of the back were fake.

However, *Batman* star Adam West obviously decided that having spent all day in such a car, he really couldn't drive home in something normal. So

the lorry was carrying a 36 ft long water tank containing six sharks and on impact the nine-foot beasts shot into a ▶

do you know what he bought as everyday transport in real life?

An Excalibur. Yes. An Excalibur, for Chrissakes. Best known as the car chosen by Mark Grayson in *Dallas* it is, without any question or shadow of doubt, the most preposterous machine ever to grace God's earth. They basically took a Corvette and threw away the only good bit – the body – which they then replaced with what they thought resembled a 1930s Mercedes. It didn't. It resembled the contents of a baby's nappy. It was indeed a rare car, in that it really was as nasty to drive as it was to behold.

JAMES GARNER – A REAL MAVERICK

We all know that Steve McQueen and Paul Newman liked to race cars in their spare time, which, of course, made them top geezers. But it is a little known fact that James Garner star of *The Great Escape* with McQueen, and *The Rockford Files*, was also fully up to speed in the art of wheelmanship.

Born in 1928, in Oklahoma he was wounded twice in Korea, which isn't terribly interesting. And nor, I guess will you be all that bothered to learn that his first job in acting saw him cueing Henry Fonda. What matters is that while McQueen was replaced by stuntmen for the trickier shots, James Garner did all his own driving in the film *Grand Prix*. He was such a petrolhead, in fact, that he regularly took part in off-road desert races and, at the age of 41, completed the ultra gruelling Mexican 1000, having driven all 832 miles himself, non-stop. One year later, in the Mint 400, he cheated death when his Oldsmobile 442 flipped at 90 mph. That year, he formed his own racing company – naming it American International Racing – which owned ten off-road vehicles and a handful of road racers, but it was folded when the corporate backing dried up.

Garner was left with nothing but two Ferraris, a Porsche and his favourite car of them all – a Mini Cooper. ⭐

car coming the other way, killing the driver. ★BIZARRE★

KEEP DEATH OFF HOLLYWOOD ROADS
(HIRE A CHAUFFEUR)

From early stone-age conflict right up to present day, war has killed a great many people. But as a killing machine, human conflict – even atomic human conflict – is second rate compared to the car, which in the blink of an eye – just 100 years – has slaughtered a staggering 25 million people. And, of course, being a machine, it knows no difference between a beautiful princess and a steel worker from Cleveland, Ohio. It kills them all, without grace or favour...

JAMES DEAN

Ever since that fateful September day in 1955, everyone has known that James Dean, star of *Rebel Without A Cause*, was killed while on the way to a race meeting in his Porsche Spyder. He was doing 85 mph when, at the intersection between Highway 46 and Highway 41, he hit a 1950 Ford Tudor being driven, rather unfortunately, by a chap called Mr Turnipspeed.

Rebel Without A Pause: what was left of James Dean's Porsche.

The left side of Dean's Porsche which had the words 'Little Bastard' in red on the boot lid, was totally destroyed in the head-on impact and Dean died instantly. His passenger – mechanic Rolf Weutherich – escaped with a broken leg and a broken arm. Mr Turnipspeed went home with nothing but a silly name. Witnesses were interviewed and after working out that weather conditions were good, police investigators said no-one was to blame and that was the end of that — but it wasn't. Not by a long way.

Shiny car. Nice gloves. Big hair. Bad Turnipseed.

After the crash, the car was bought by a friend and colleague of Dean – George Barris – who planned to sell it bit by bit, part by part. He paid $2,500 and towed the car 200 miles to his workshop in Southern California where, as it was being unloaded from the truck, it fell and landed on a mechanic, breaking both his legs. The spookiest story in the whole history of motoring was underway.

Barris eventually sold the engine to a Beverly Hills doctor who raced cars at weekends. But not for much longer. In the first race of the year while driving the car into which he'd fitted Dean's engine, he went out of control, hit a tree and was killed. In the same race, another doctor was seriously injured when his car rolled. He had been using the drivetrain from Dean's Porsche.

So what of the tyres then? Well, they were sold to a sports car driver who, just a week later, phoned to say that two had blown out at the same time and for no good reason. The car had ended up off the road, where investigators said the rubber was in good condition and that the double blow-out was a complete mystery. By this time, the Highway Patrol had decided to use what was left of Dean's car to tour the country where it would be used to urge teenage drivers to slow down.

Barris welded the body work together and the car set off. But three weeks later it was back, having been stored overnight in a building that had suddenly caught fire and burned down. As had the building next door. Once again, Barris botched up the bent and singed car and sent it off to complete the tour. And once again, it fell off a transporter, breaking an onlooker's hip. Then, three weeks later, it was loaded on a truck for transportation to Salinas – the exact same town where Dean was headed on the night he was killed. And guess what, the truck driver was killed in a freak accident.

Two years later, the Porsche fell off the back of a lorry, causing a city centre pile-up. In Oregon, the truck on which it was mounted slipped its emergency brake and smashed into a store. In New Orleans, while resting on steel supports, it fell into eleven pieces. And then in 1960, while in the hands of the Florida Highway Patrol it simply disappeared... and it's never been heard of since. But the people it touched continued to make news. In 1968, Rolf Weutherich, the mechanic who'd been with Dean on the night he was killed, was convicted of murdering his wife. ★

YOU'RE ONLY SUPPOSED TO BLOW THE BLOODY DOORS OFF

When it comes to opening sequences, any film which has already employed a bulldozer to bludgeon the world's most beautiful car into nothing more than a wheelbarrow-load of brightly-painted bent bits before you've even remembered that your girlfriend is actually sitting to your right and the popcorn you're easily half way through belongs to a complete stranger, merits, at the very least, the accolade 'Promising'. But, in the 1969 film classic *The Italian Job*, the best was yet to come. The masticated Lamborghini Miura proved to be little more than an automotive *amuse bouche*. Not even Noel Coward's upper-class, indifferently imprisoned mastermind, nor Michael Caine's gently bewildered 'You're only supposed to blow the bloody doors off!' Cockney could outshine the real star of the show – a Union Jack of hyperactive Mini Coopers putting Turin traffic to the sword and the instant ownership of a Mini on the wish list of every red-blooded male in Great Britain.

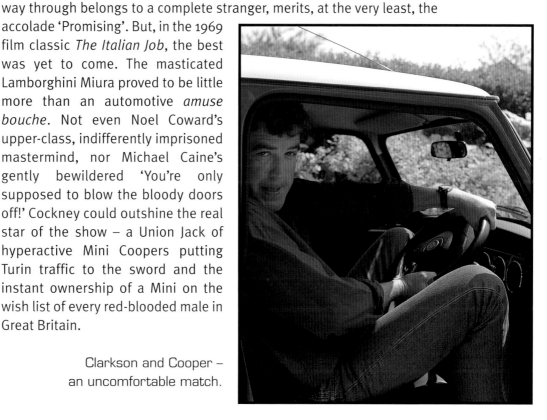

Clarkson and Cooper –
an uncomfortable match.

On the 26th of August 1999, designer Sir Alec Issigonis' remarkable blob will roll out the party hats, make merry with the Hundreds and Thousands and rightly demand large, wrapped gifts from all its friends for the 40th time. With only the possible exception of a certain German jelly-mould, no other car on the planet has ever come close to matching the Mini's visually unchanged longevity, or its appeal.

MY TOP 20 DRIVES

THE CAR	Silverstone to London. BMW M5.
THE PLACE	Silverstone to London.
THE DRIVER . . .	A well-known touring car racer.
THE MEMORY . .	It took 21 minutes!

The fact that this little car has survived, more or less intact save for a dreadful new interior, the hopeless ministrations of Austin, Morris, BMC, British Leyland, Leyland Cars, BL, BL Cars, Austin Morris and Austin Rover, in that order, is reason enough to roll out the bunting. And there's a strange sibling symmetry to the fact that, as part of the Rover Group, the Mini is now in BMW's hands; Sir Alec Issigonis' mother is the sister of the grandmother of BMW chairman, Bernd Pischetsrieder, who has described it as 'the only loveable car on the road'.

Which has always been the Mini's secret weapon: owners, even those who couldn't give a panty liner for things on four wheels, have always fallen head-over-heels in love with it. Issigonis said he styled the Mini so that it could never be obsolescent. But, in creating a round, cuddly shape with all the vulnerable appeal of an over-hugged teddy-bear, he also offered a motoring world awash with bearded, stuffy adult barges in black tail-coats the secret of eternal youth. For this is a car that never grew up. A child. And, because it's never been thought of as an adult, that fact that it's cramped, noisy and uncomfortable is taken for granted and, more importantly, forgiven. Furthermore, in the same way that young children haven't yet assimilated the class values and ideals of their parents, the Mini was to defy clear categorisation in the pavement pecking order and become the world's only classless car. Although not without a struggle...

At it's launch on August 26th 1959, the Mini cost £496. The cheapest

★**BIZARRE** *5. When Franz Hassel's ancient Beetle wouldn't start, he decided to bump start it by pushing the old*

British-built rival of the day was the following year's Ford Popular; a shrunken version of the stuffy, adult barge available at a bargain £419. The Anglia was 4 mph faster than the Mini, offering a face-bending 76 mph. with the fully flattened mushroom, and half a second quicker, at 16.5 seconds, to 60 mph. But in the handling stakes, the Anglia stood as much chance against the Mini as a goose on ice. Issigonis had an idyllic notion of a Mini outside every woodman's cottage. But, in truth, the car had to wait a decade and half until it was itself a teenager in the mid-1970s, before attracting the young, low income, first-time buyer of Issigonis' dreams. Initially, the Mini's price difference with the Anglia put off the poorest buyers. And the middle classes either got a better bargain than they should have – doing nothing for company profits – or dismissed the car as being too cheap to be worthy of them. Which only left the toffs in the running. The Mini had already gained the royal seal of approval from day one, when Issigonis took the Queen for a spin around Hyde Park in his creation. However, success only truly arrived with the Mini's adoption by the hip and heavy-walleted city folk.

The Americans saw fit to invent the teenager in the 1950s as a post-war celebration of all things US of A. Up to that point, we were all running about the shop as spotty, short-trousered clones of our parents. But, awash with a surfeit of recreational drugs and ridiculous trousers, it was the London of the late 1960s that fast became the 'happening' capital of the world. And this revolution in music, fashion and the arts prompted a previously undreamed of class crossover. With the likes of The Stones, The Who and The Beatles all coining it, the capital became a heady cocktail of East End lads and aristocrats revelling in the rejection of past values. And money. Mick Jagger became mates with the likes of Lord Snowdon, and Vidal Sassoon stopped beating the crap out of Moseley's Blackshirts to concentrate on, um, hairdressing.

banger along a mountain road near his home in Austria. Once the car was rolling he tried to jump in and take the ▶

Even Italian car washes have more style.

When it came to wheels, the Mini fitted the bill perfectly. No member of a popular beat combo wanted the status symbols of the fuddy-duddy generation. John Lennon only got away with Rolls ownership by painting every inch of the thing in all available colours while under the influence of substances not available in shops. The injection of added fizz at the hands of John Cooper gave the Mini a further nudge towards cult status and provided yet another opportunity for the British to rub the French up the wrong way. Starting with Paddy Hopkirk's famous win in 1964, the car so dominated their showcase motorsport event, the Monte Carlo Rally, as to cause a beef of BSE proportions. Finally, after a spectacular 1-2-3 victory in 1966, French officials had had enough and spent eight hours scrabbling around the cars before coming up with a disqualification on the most dubious of technicalities – the wrong headlight bulbs.

Having thus earned a reputation as a sports car, the Mini immediately came under attack from the beard brigade. Newspapers were full of quotes from professors and policemen who branded it 'conducive to inconsiderate driving'. Mini owners, meanwhile, unable to master the phonetic spelling of a loud and hectoring raspberry, sported rear stickers announcing 'You've Just Been Mini'd'. In later years, a number of police forces were obliged to use the Mk2 Cooper S as a patrol car, on the basis that it took one to catch one.

wheel, but the door handle came off in his hand and Franz could only watch as the car shot over the cliff, plunging

Nope, didn't leave the Cooper there.

The Aga Khan and Steve McQueen bought Coopers. A fistful of racing drivers, including Graham Hill, Bruce McLaren and John Surtees, couldn't resist the car, and even Enzo Ferrari had one (well, three actually) in which he took to the hills above Modena when he wanted some fun. Lord Snowdon bought one and had a wind-up window fitted to his side of the car, keeping the standard, sliding window on Princess Margaret's side because it buggered up her hairdo a sight less. Twiggy murdered her consonants behind the wheel of a Mini and, if we're to believe the story, Mary Quant's inspiration through ownership set about raising hem-lines to previously undreamed of heights. So much so that it rapidly became possible to establish what most girls had eaten for breakfast without the blush and bother of asking them.

But it was the film industry that was to finally saturate our senses with the Mini and, after a decidedly shaky start, guarantee its success. Peter Sellers was given a Mini on his birthday in 1965 by his (then) wife Britt Ekland, who still drives one today. Brigitte Bardot, David Niven, Paul Newman, Dudley Moore, Norman Wisdom, Clint Eastwood, er, Tommy Steele – all were seduced by the Mini's image. Not to mention what it could do for their own...

By the time *The Italian Job* hit the popcorn emporia in 1969, the public knew more about the Mini through the stars who drove them than through the cinema itself. But a selection of outrageous, rooftop-to-rain-sewer stunts put together by Remy Julienne in one of the all-time-great getaway movie scenes soon rectified that, and that most classless of all entertainments, the cinema, gave the classless Mini a wider audience than ever before. But it still wasn't until the Mini had been around for 18 years, that anyone actually thought to market it properly. 'Small' was out; the word was 'Fun'. 'Happiness is Mini shaped' was the new slogan, and Twiggy, Lulu and Spike Milligan all pitched in with TV advertising

into a holiday chalet 150 ft below. Nobody was at home, but the owners sued Mr Hassel for £157,000. ★BIZARRE

49

'The bill – leg it!' Not many people know this; *The Italian Job* had a very small budget.

MY TOP 20 DRIVES

THE CAR . . . . . . *Subaru Impreza Turbo.*

THE PLACE . . . . *Autosports Show,*
NEC, Birmingham.

THE DRIVER . . . *Happy-go-lucky*
Colin McRae.

THE MEMORY . . *The fastest doughnuts it is*
possible to do, according
to the laws of physics.
Go any quicker and you
end up in 1489.

'No, I told you girl, the bloody producers have got to pay the bill.'

campaigns. By 1976 the average age of car ownership had dropped dramatically, and the number of women owners was rocketing. No longer was rapid and dramatic transport the exclusive preserve of the rich; the young and impecunious sons of the soil could finally fulfil Issigonis' aspirations for them in a Mini.

Coincidentally, this little car also instigated the biggest boom in car accessories that there's ever been. Personalisation of private transport simply took off with the Mini: wheel spacers; fog lamps; go-faster stripes; non-slip accelerator pedal extensions for heel and toe enthusiasts; inside lower door kick-plates to prevent winkle-pickers tearing the trim (honest); and even those three-inch, flexible plastic extendaswitches that I used to so love testing to destruction. Though, in truth, they were a necessity; you couldn't reach the originals if you wore a seat belt...

Once again, though, it was a film star who started the ball rolling. Peter Sellers, with his famous wickerwork-flanked specimen, was perhaps the most famous Mini fan of all: 'For anyone between 25 and 45, the Mini was part of growing up,' he said in 1979. 'It gave mobility to millions and bankrupted the textile mills by leading the way to mini-skirts (sigh). For thousands of us who had to get around London quickly, the Mini was like the answer to a prayer. We stuck wickerwork on the sides, rushed it up to Oxford Circus and caned it down Park Lane.'

Mercifully, the Mini survived both those appalling puns and, to date, some 5.3 million have been made. Park that little lot end to end, and the queue would stretch from London to Sydney. But the end is nigh. And, for those of you lucky enough to find yourselves suffering from fat wallet syndrome, here's a little investment tip: shares in Kleenex will go through the roof in the year 2003. New crash test regulations from nanny Brussels will finally lay the Mini, 44 years old by then, to rest. And there won't be a dry eye on the planet. ★

INTRODUCING THE NEWEST STAR IN...

HOLLYWOOD

MR RANGE ROVER

Hollywood stars demand and get the best of everything, but for some strange reason they've fallen in love with the Range Rover. On the streets of Beverly Hills, where fads move faster than Clinton's secretaries, Solihull's finest has become more of an institution than Burt Reynold's wig. Here are just some of the names in Range Rover log books. Deep breath:

★ **Cher** ★ **Harry Connick Jnr** ★ **Tom Cruise** ★ **Michael Douglas**
Joe Esterhaus ★ **Emilio Estevez** ★ **Robert Evans** ★ **Peter Falk**
Jane Fonda ★ **Michael J Fox** ★ **Dustin Hoffman** ★ **Whitney Houston**
Timothy Hutton ★ **Julio Iglesias** ★ **Janet Jackson** ★ **Michael Jackson**
Don Johnson ★ **Magic Johnson** ★ **Quincy Jones** ★ **Estee Lauder**
Ivan Lendl ★ **Barry Manilow** ★ **John McVie (Fleetwood Mac)**
George Michael ★ **Mary Tyler Moore** ★ **Jack Nicholson** ★ **Greg Norman**
Stephanie Powers ★ **Priscilla Presley** ★ **Lionel Ritchie** ★ **Kenny Rogers**
Sissy Spacek ★ **Rod Stewart** ★ **Sting** ★ **Donna Summer Patrick Swayze**
Mike Tyson ★ **Tracey Ullman** ★ **Eddie Van Halen** ★ **Robert Wagner**
Bruce Willis ★ **Oprah Winfrey** ★ **Debra Winger** ★ **John Kettlee**

Land Rover's biggest Hollywood coup, however, happened not recently, but some time in the 23rd Century. In the Sylvester Stallone movie *Judge Dredd*, Land Rover managed to grab the starring role as the only vehicles tough enough to survive in the lawless 23rd Century. Unfortunately, the film was a complete pile of dog's droppings, but Land Rover got the exposure they wanted. Even the car stylists at Solihull managed to get one over on the all powerful Hollywood set designers: having seen the Hollywood drawings for the Land Rover of the future, the Brummies pooh-poohed the yank efforts and came up with their own sketches. Arguments ensued between the two camps, until the film's director walked in, looked at the Solihull offering and said, 'Give me 25 of those.' ★

MUSIC & MODELLING

Rock 'n' roll came along at exactly the same moment that cars started to hunker down and get sleek. And the two have been joined at the hip ever since. Musical success provided young men with the ability to buy whatever car took their fancy and, if they wished, to drive that car into a swimming pool. Or a tree. Musicians have penned songs about cars, drawn inspiration from cars and lost limbs in their cars. Today, the car is an integral part of a thousand pop videos and music is an integral part of the supercar success story. Were it not for music, Ferrari and Lamborghini would have folded back in the days when Janis Joplin was praying, 'Oh Lord, won't you buy me a Mercedes Benz?'

HEAVY METAL THUNDER

Twenty years ago my schoolboy logic was adamant that every rock star had a Lamborghini. There were, of course, a few exceptions: Supertramp were too busy growing kidney beans; Keith Richards was travelling, not necessarily in the sense you and I understand, but by his own special form of transport; and Keith Moon was too drunk to find the dealership. But for anyone else with the ability to earn an enormous crust by arranging the words, 'girl', 'baby', 'thing', 'hot', 'down', 'tonight' and 'sausage' in various orders, surely the Italian equivalent of Robert Plant's hosepipe was the only suitable car. Lamborghinis are ostentatious, yes, vulgar even, but no heavy metal crooner, lying on his death bed and looking back on his life, ever uttered the words: 'Thank God I didn't shag that convent.' Sadly though, a trawl

★BIZARRE *6. A 14-year-old German girl took her father's car out for a midnight drive and wrote it off when she*

through the Lamborghini archives reveals a rather meagre selection of rockers have put their X in a Lambo log book. There was Rod Stewart – a very loyal customer, with a Miura, Countach and Diablo – Paul McCartney with an Espada, Black Sabbath axeman Tony Iommi, who owned a Miura, and, er, that's it. Soppy pop group Five Star, England's answer to the Jacksons, had a couple of Countaches in the late 1980s, but they went bankrupt when they tried to fill them up with petrol.

One problem is that the seriously walleted rock star car lovers, such as Mark Knopfler and Nick Mason, prefer restoring cars to crashing them, and Lambos are just not their bag. However, there is now light at the end of the dressing room tunnel, as the Lambo creeps back into fashion with '90s rock stars such as Jay Kay and Toby Smith from Jamiroquai – owners, respectively, of a Diablo SV and a 1976 flatside Countach 400 – and The Prodigy's Liam Howlett, who also drives a Diablo SV. It's good to see that at long last, the world of rock 'n' roll is starting to take Lamborghini seriously. I mean, they were made for each other. And here's why...

I live way out in the countryside, which is supposed to be quiet and peaceful and relaxing. But it isn't. As I sit at night, working at my computer

Opposite: McCartney and Mini in 1966. Above: Sir Cliff Richard, yesterday.

crashed into a tree. However, in court the judge ruled that the girl could not be prosecuted for wrecking the car ▶

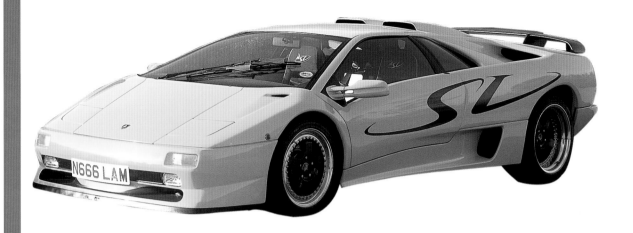

Robert Plant and Jimmy Page take a breather. Oh sorry. It's a Diablo.

until the wee small hours, the house echoes to strange and worrying sounds. Upstairs, the wisteria taps rhythmically on a window pane and down below, in the basement, a boiler made by the Boers ticks as it cools. Every now and again, the outdoor security lights illuminate the garden for no obvious reason and then, seconds later, there will be a thump coming from somewhere near the back door. For 18 years, I lived in London and I wasn't scared once, but every night out here, at some point I'll be creeping round the house, bathed in sweat as I search for imagined intruders. Last week though, I nearly messed my pants.

It started as a distant rumble way off over the fields and just got louder and louder. There's no way it was a plane, for two reasons: it was coming toward me too slowly to be a jet and it had to be a jet to be making that much noise; but then as its lights swung into the drive, I realised that no jet makes a sound quite like this. No engine I've ever heard is quite so bassy, quite so rich and terrifying. No human could have made such a thing. By the time it had slithered into the courtyard, the dog was eating its own tail in fear and the children were awake and crying – hysterical, open mouthed screaming, their eyes wide in terror.

It turned out to be a friend of mine who'd dropped by in a Lamborghini Diablo SV – the new one, with more horsepower and a sports exhaust – the noisy one. It looks pretty much the same as any other Diablo and though it is able to crack 200 mph, it is not really that much faster. The sound, though, is quite extraordinary. Imagine sticking your head into a lion's mouth and amplifying the noise through the Grateful Dead's speaker

or driving without a licence because she was sleepwalking throughout the whole incident. After the crash, the girl

system, and you'd be nowhere near even the same ball park. Hell, you wouldn't even be in the same county. This car is Led Zeppelin on wheels.

We are familiar today with heavy metal – a curious mixture of beseeching ballads and balls-out, ear-splitting noise. There are Guns N' Roses, Metallica, Def Leppard and a thousand more, all of whom can trace their roots back to one band – Led Zeppelin. If heavy metal can be likened to a species, these guys were the amoebas. No matter how many drinks Liam Gallagher manages to spill on aeroplane flights to Australia, he is just a pale imitation of the Led Zep boys. Led Zep weren't conforming to a prearranged, stage-managed set of rules – they were inventing it as they went along. They were very young and very rich and very drunk, so that if they suddenly felt the need to ride a motorbike through the hotel, they just did. I have always wanted to throw a television from a hotel bedroom window – power sliding across a golf course is all I want to do more – but instead of sitting around thinking about it, John Bonham just unplugged the Grundig, cried havoc and let slip the electric fish tank.

And when they checked out, the band simply peeled off enough extra notes to cover the damage, famously thrusting an extra hundred into a hotel manager's sweaty palms with the immortal line, 'Have one on us.' Moments later, as they climbed into the limo, they turned to see the said manager atop the roof, thanking them profusely as he hurled a TV set into the garden 14 storeys down.

Give Led Zep a Rolls Royce and they'd put it in the swimming pool. Give them a hotel suite and they'd wreck it. They were 20 years old and they had their own BAC1-11. It just didn't matter. And then, that night they'd be on stage blasting out their strange new musical mix at the sort of volume that would make your ears bleed. I was never a fan of the band but I saw them once at Knebworth,

had knocked on the door of a nearby house and told the owner: 'I dreamt I was driving a car.' She then fell down ▶

MY TOP 20 DRIVES

THE CAR	Well it was an F15 jet, actually.
THE PLACE	North Carolina, USA.
THE DRIVER . . .	Captain Dave Grimwald.
THE MEMORY . .	A curious mixture of G-forces and vomit.

and it was truly epic. Led Zeppelin/Lamborghini Diablo. Lamborghini Diablo/Led Zeppelin. Same thing.

You see, Led Zep may have started a trend but the founder, guitarist Jimmy Page, had come from the Yardbirds who were very much entrenched in the world of R&B. And it's much the same story with Lamborghini. The founder – Ferruccio Lamborghini – started out making front-engined GT cars to rival other front-engined GT cars from Maserati, Alfa Romeo and most of all, Ferrari. Had he continued down this route, he would have gone down the tubes years ago.

But he didn't. In 1966, he gave us the Miura, the first mid engined road car and all of a sudden, he was ahead of the game. His Led Zep II moment came with the Countach but there's no doubt that his 'Stairway To Heaven' – his crowning achievement – was the Diablo. This was the car that established his company as the greatest purveyor of automotive heavy metal the world has ever seen. While Lotus and Ferrari have experimented with glam rock and prog rock and even punk, Lamborghini has never given up on simple, big-engined, big cars with big power and big wheels. Heavy Metal.

It's worth noting here, too, that I have the same relationship with the Diablo as I do with Led Zep. It may be a terrific spectacle but I'm not really a fan. I'd always choose a Ferrari instead, but that said I'm always prepared to give it a go. And so on that dark and spooky night, I slithered into the deep, body-form seat, fired up the biblical 5.7 litre V12 and headed out into the night. The headlamps popped out of that stubby bonnet and for a while I dawdled, reacquainting myself with the notion of 530 bhp, 450 ft lbs of

on the porch and had to be taken to hospital to be woken by doctors. ★BIZARRE★

torque and brakes which take you from 70 mph to a standstill in a mere 169 feet. It didn't take long and with that sports exhaust hammering the hedgerows, the temptation was too much, so a mile down the road I buried the throttle... and started to live. Thirty to seventy mph took just 3.46 seconds and then the V12 was really into its stride; 13 seconds later, I was past 140 and still there was no let up. This SV, the stripped out, cheapskate two wheel drive Diablo – the cheapest in the range – shot past the 200 mph mark.

Now this, I hasten to add, was on a tame airfield round these parts – I know of no road in Britain where 200 mph is realistic and that really is the Diablo's shortcoming. Asking it to perform on a normal A road is like asking Led Zep to perform at the Mean Fiddler. Sure, the Diablo with its garden roller tyres has enough grip to break your neck but it doesn't have the delicacy of a 355 or Lotus Esprit. It can be flowing and graceful in the same way that a heavy metal band can do ballads, but you are always waiting for the epic finale to the song, the moment when those four camshafts really start to work for a living. Drive a car like this in the right place, and at the right time, and your shadow really will be taller than your soul. Drive it in the wrong place at the wrong time, and there'll be rather more than a bustle in your hedgerow. ★

I SHOULD WRITE

THE SONGS WHICH SELL THE CARS

Using well-known music to promote a new model is nothing new, but actually matching the right track to the right car would be something of a novelty. I mean, Peugeot gave us 'Search For The Hero Inside Yourself', which was jolly catchy and so on, but really it was wasted somewhat on that repmobile 406. And what on earth were Rover thinking about when they bought Sting another trout lake. 'An Englishman In New York' would have been fine, but after several catastrophic attempts Rover is no longer marketed in America.

Ford, for Christ's sake, once used the Bill Withers classic 'Sunshine Day' to promote the Escort. Well, one thing's for damn sure; if you had to drive around in that heap of nonsense, it sure as hell wasn't going to be a bright, bright, bright sunshiney day. It was going to be a grey, grey, grey, dull day. Here, then, are my suggestions for what song should go with what car:

Eric Clapton as 'Willie'. BMW 318i his 'Hand Jive'.

'Hope I die before I get a Volvo.' Get an Alfa 156, Rog, don't get fooled again.

1 **The Who** ★ **'Won't Get Fooled Again'** ★ **Alfa Romeo 156**
2 Led Zep ★ 'Stairway To Heaven' ★ Lamborghini Diablo
3 **Tina Turner** ★ **'Simply The Best'** ★ **Ferrari 355**
4 Squeeze ★ 'Cool For Cats' ★ Jaguar XJR
5 **Pink Floyd** ★ **'Shine On You Crazy Diamond'** ★ **Aston Martin Vantage**
6 Underworld ★ 'Born Slippy' ★ Porsche 911 Turbo
7 **Pulp** ★ **'Common People'** ★ **Ford Escort**
8 Eels ★ 'Novocaine For The Soul' ★ Vauxhall Astra
9 **Iggy Pop** ★ **'Lust For Life'** ★ **Lotus Elise**
10 Belinda Carlisle ★ 'Heaven Is A Place On Earth' ★ Bentley Arnage
11 **Eric Clapton** ★ **'Willy And The Hand Jive'** ★ **BMW 318i**
12 The Korgis ★ 'Everybody's Gotta Learn Sometime' ★ Sinclair C5
13 **ELO** ★ **'Hold On Tight'** ★ **Peugeot 106GTi**
14 Richard Marx ★ 'Hazard' ★ Nissan Almera
15 **Robert Plant** ★ **'Big Log'** ★ **Vauxhall Vectra**
16 Eddie & The Hot Rods ★ 'Do Anything You Wanna Do' ★ Nissan Skyline GTR
17 **Tears For Fears** ★ **'Everybody Wants To Rule The World'** ★ **Mercedes S Class**
18 INXS ★ 'Elegantly Wasted' ★ Ferrari 456
19 **Paul Weller** ★ **'The Changingman'** ★ **Volvo T5**
20 Sheryl Crow ★ 'Every Day Is A Winding Road' ★ Ford Puma

The spot where Bolan went to sit behind the big steering wheel in the sky.

ONE CRASH TO HEAVEN

THE TOP TEN ROCK 'N' ROLL AUTOMOBILE ACCIDENTS

1. MARC BOLAN

On September 16, 1977 Bolan was being driven through Barnes by his girlfriend, backing singer Gloria Jones, in a purple Mini 1275GT when it hit a tree. Jones was seriously injured and Bolan died. That pretty much was the end of T. Rex, but more tragedies were to come. Four years later, at the age of 31, the band's co-founder Steve Took choked and died. And 12 months later, at the age of just 34, bassist Steve Curry died, too.

2. EDDIE COCHRAN

Famous for hits like 'Summertime Blues' and 'C'mon Everybody', Cochran was enormously popular in Britain – so popular that his 1960 tour of the UK was elongated from five to fifteen weeks. But he became homesick and ordered a taxi to take him to Heathrow for a flight back to the States. On the A4 just outside Bath, a tyre blew and the car hit a lamppost. He really was on those three steps to Heaven.

★BIZARRE *7. Tourist Harold Womack accidentally drove his £36,000 Porsche into a pit while visiting Sunset*

3. ROB COLLINS

The former keyboard player for Oxford's Charlatans never had much luck with cars. At the end of 1992, having popped out for a beer with a mate, Collins found himself driving the getaway motor in an armed robbery. He served eight months in prison for the offence. Two years after his release from prison in 1994, Collins died on his way to hospital after his car veered out of control, hit several parked vehicles and ended up in a field.

MY TOP 20 DRIVES

THE CAR . . . . . . Ferrari 355.
THE PLACE . . . . Tuscany, Italy.
THE DRIVER . . . Me.
THE MEMORY . . I have discovered motoring perfection.

4. COZY POWELL

The rock drummer who played with a number of bands including Black Sabbath and had a couple of solo hits in the early 1970s, died in his Saab early in 1998. No other cars were involved in the accident. Now he really is 'Dancing With The Devil'.

5. ALAN BARTON

Smokie's former frontman is no longer 'Living Next Door To Alice'; he died in a Cologne hospital in 1995. Five members of the band were injured, and Barton left in a coma for six days after their bus skidded and overturned during a hailstorm on the way to a gig in Dusseldorf, Germany.

6. RICK ALLEN

The drummer with Sheffield's heavy metal gods Def Leppard lost his left arm after turning his AC Cobra over several times while attempting to take a corner. He went on to continue his long and successful career .

7. BRYAN ADAMS

The Canadian rocker responsible for clogging up the charts for the summer of 1991 with the cloying goo that was 'Everything I Do (I Do It For You)', cheated death when a French woman driving a Peugeot 205 skidded into his Range Rover while he was touring France in July 1992. She was killed.

Crater National Monument in Arizona. The 30-year-old businessman realised he would be stranded for hours in ▶

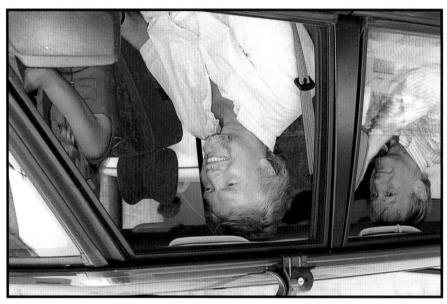

Richard Branson and his Range Rover in an off-road moment.

8. RICHARD BRANSON

The former Virgin records chief bought a fleet of Range Rovers after his own Vogue rolled on the M4. The great man says he would have been killed had he been in any other car. But Richard, ask yourself this simple question. Would any other car have rolled in the first place?

9. BOYZONE

After hearing that Shane and Keith had rolled a Golf GTi while (allegedly) doing 90 mph in 1995, the band's record company banned them from driving quickly. Er, how would they know?

10. HUGH WHITAKER

Once drummer with self-professed second best band in Hull, The Housemartins, Mr Whitaker wasn't actually involved in a crash, but is currently serving a sentence in prison because of a car. At the height of the band's success, Mr Whitaker invested some money in a second-hand car dealership which went wrong. After failing (twice) to set fire to his former partner's house, he finally banged on his door and attacked him with a machête. Mr Whitaker was jailed for six years in May 1993. ★

the remote spot over 60 miles from the nearest town, but thought his problems were over when he spotted a 20 ton

Left: Elle
MacPherson –
no chance of The
Body rusting.
Right: Kate Moss,
viewed from the
side.

WHY SUPERMODELS DON'T DRIVE

I don't think I've ever seen a supermodel driving a car. I've seen photographs of them lounging on cars, and paparazzi shots of them climbing out of cars but not once, not ever, have I seen one actually driving. This is weird. I mean, we're forever being told that these girls won't get out of bed for less than £10,000, which means, presumably, they're well enough rested to have the energy for driving a car. And we must assume also they're easily rich enough to have a fairly tasty set of wheels on the driveway.

Largely, they don't drink much either. I have, for instance, never seen Claudia Schiffer in my boozer downing ten pints with whiskey chasers. But I have been to a party where I noted Kate Moss sipping on what looked like

road roller left unattended by workmen. Harold drove the roller to the edge of the pit and then hopped out to ▶

The Vauxhall Campbell and the Austin Moss – good little runarounds.

lettuce-flavoured mineral water. I'm sure she could have driven home legally but she climbed instead into a taxi – with her knees together. Sadly.

There was a time, of course, when cars were distinctly un-hip, when it would have been more appropriate to discover that Elle MacPherson had a train set than to find out that she had an Allegro. But not any more. Today, there are any number of super-trendy and affordable sports cars which would fit the bill just fine. The Porsche Boxster, for instance, is right up there with a Prada frock. And even the MGF cuts the ice with the aplomb of lunch at the Bluebird Cafe. And come on. If these girls really are on ten grand a day, they only need a ten day photo shoot to pay for a Ferrari 355. And if a supermodel in a Ferrari doesn't get your stuff going, your stuff isn't working. I only need consider the concept and I'm overwhelmed with a sudden need to visit the lavatory.

So why then are these girls never seen behind the wheel? Some suggest that after dieting for years on nothing but celery and grass, washed down

attach a chain to the Porsche so he could pull it out. Do I really need to finish this...? ★BIZARRE★

68

with lettuce-flavoured water, they simply don't have the strength to press the pedals or turn the wheel. But this is nonsense. I have arms and legs like pipe cleaners, and I can manage. I last took some exercise in 1977 and was staggered to discover the other day I had pulled a muscle. I really didn't know I had any left.

Sure, a Lamborghini Diablo would be something of a struggle for the thin-limbed but we're talking here about a power-steered, hydraulically-assisted Boxster, not a photocopier-wrestling competition.

You know what I think? I think supermodels do drive, but because they're so thin, we can't see them doing it. So, the next time you're behind a car which appears to have no one in the driver's seat, don't assume the driver is 100 years old and has shrunk below the level of the headrest. Consider this. You could be following Jodie Kidd.

Kate Moss tucks into a healthy lunch seemingly comprising several different liquids.

WHITHER THE SUPERMODEL?

Since it was decided to heap praise and money on women with bodies like bamboo shoots and breasts like fried eggs, we have learned a great deal about supermodels. We know the names of their boyfriends. We know what they wear under their dresses. And while broadsheet newspapers run court circulars to keep us up to date on what the royals are doing, the red tops run a sort of court shoe circular to let us know who'll be at what film premiere.

It is now impossible to turn on a satellite television channel without finding a fly on the wall documentary about 'the making of a supermodel'. And so we know exactly what the talent scouts are looking for. We know the top lips mustn't be too thin and that the breasts have to be inverted. We know that nine is really the upper age-limit and that eyes on the side of the head, rather than the front, are a good idea, too. Some kind of drug dependency is essential, as is an allergy to all food stuffs that aren't lettuce or celery-based. And rather than dressing up to go out, the supermodel-in-the-making must dress down to the point where either she is naked, or looks like something from Steptoe's cart. No girl, no matter how huge her head and how long her legs, stands an earthly unless she looks like she's washed her hair in glue and then dipped it in a used Hoover bag. But most important of all, she must have a temper, an ability to turn the air blue, even in confessional.

Supermodels are rich and fragile and when you add these two ingredients together, it is like splitting the atom. You've got a bomb that'll go off if it's a bit windy outside, or if the lettuce isn't Cos. And so it goes with supercars. The first and most important ingredient of a supercar is that it must have no space inside for a driver, a passenger or anything that might be considered luggage. It must also hug the ground to the point that any form of kerb, raised manhole cover or debris will completely remove the nose section, causing thousands of pounds worth of damage.

Then there's the engine, which must refuse to start in the morning unless you give it a £10,000 service. And you can't just feed it on any old fuel – it insists on having diamond-encrusted super unleaded which comes with free myrrh from only two petrol stations in the country. To drive, the controls must be heavy and cumbersome and if you take a corner even slightly off line, the back will swing round, causing even more damage. Supercars then, like supermodels, are petulant and awkward. They're hard to drive, hard to live with and hard to understand. We forgive them though because they look like angels and go like rabbits.

Look at it this way. You're married to a lovely girl who has a great job, and a degree in oral sex and cooking. But you crave a night out with a supermodel even though she won't eat and will want to be in bed, on her own, at 9.30 pm. You drive a Ford Escort but you crave a Ferrari F40, even though you know in your heart of hearts it'll break down, crash and get vandalised every time you stop moving. We crave them because they're dream cars. And what we have here are the five most likely to wake you up in the middle of the night, wrapped in damp sheets... ⭐

⭐**BIZARRE** *8. Batsman Andrew Tynan was cheered by his team when he hit a six during a local cricket match. But*

70

SUPER MODELS & SUPERMODELS

1. MCLAREN F1

I never did a review of the McLaren F1, for which I shall be eternally grateful. You see, had I been asked to take a cold-hearted, clinical look, I'd have been acutely aware that some of the people reading could afford a million dollar hypercar. And so I would have needed to temper whatever enthusiasm I had for its speed and handling with a quest for objectivity. In short, I'd have been out there, trying to find out whether it really was worth six times more than a Ferrari 355. To which the answer, I suspect, is no.

There are other problems, too. I felt that by moving into road car production, McLaren was taking its eye off Grand Prix racing and I think

Andrew, though, was rather less enthusiastic, as he watched the ball sail into the car park and smash straight ▶

I was right. Since they folded the F1 project, their race cars are once again the machines to beat.

Still, looking back, I have to hand out credit where credit is due and let's face it, the McLaren F1 was the fastest car ever made. With a proven top speed of 231 mph, it smashed the previous record held by Jaguar's 217 mph XJ220. And it was a superb piece of packaging. By putting the driver in the middle, there was room for two passenger seats and space for suitcases, too, in a brace of side pods which, together, gave you more luggage space than you get in a Fiesta. Sure, by being in the centre, the driver couldn't reach out of the window at motorway toll booths but, hey, this is a supercar remember. Practicality doesn't matter.

MY TOP 20 DRIVES

THE CAR. . . . . . Chevrolet Impala.
THE PLACE . . . . Havana, Cuba.
THE DRIVER . . . Me.
THE MEMORY . . This was Che Guevara's own personal car and I was the first person to drive it since his death. I'd gone just two miles when it caught fire.

What does matter are ultimates and the F1 had that little corner of the market all sewn up. Not only was it the fastest car ever made but it was just also about the most awesome to drive... if you knew what you were doing. So prodigious was the power from its 6.1 litre BMW V12 engine that in any gear at nearly any speed, your right foot could be used to break traction at the rear. And look at that shape. It had a stubby tail which was good news aesthetically and for reasons of lightness, but aerodynamically it was a nightmare. You didn't have air flow pressing the driven tyres into the road which meant that, at high speed, the handling was more nervous than

through the windscreen of his own Ford Orion. ★BIZARRE★

a lion tamer who's just inadvertently trodden on his charge's tail.

The F1s they raced at Le Mans grew huge protuberances on the back to aid stability but the road car driver just had to be quick and good. It scared the hell out of me but Tiff Needell thought it was more entertaining than setting fire to a fireworks factory. He loved it even more than he loves parties. And Tiff really, really loves parties.

I think my basic problem with this car is rather subtle. When I talk about it, I mention the technology and the cleverness rather than simply dribbling. Ask me about a Ferrari and I'll wax lyrical for hours in a voice that just gets squeakier and squeakier. But ask me about the McLaren and in solemn tones I'll tell you it had magnesium wheels, aluminium alloy brakes and titanium exhausts which weighed 67 kilos less than their steel equivalents. I'll even add that the tool kit was made

SUPERMODEL EQUIVALENT
Margaret Thatcher – powerful, British, unmanageable.

from titanium, too. You will nod sagely as I go on to tell you that as gold is the best reflector of heat, the engine bay is lined with the stuff and I'll add anecdotally that the designer, Gordon Murray, asked BMW to make the V12 weigh no more than 250 kilos. It came in 16 kilos overweight but as he'd asked for just 550 bhp, and it actually developed 627 bhp, he never complained. Then there's the suspension, which has grand plane sheer centre subframes at the front and inclined sheer axis at the back. And what about the styling? Nice. Eye catching. Noticeable. About what you'd expect from Peter Stevens, the man who brought you the Jaguar XJR15 and the Lotus Elan. But it doesn't melt the heart in the same way that a Ferrari can.

It has nothing to do with the pedigree either. Sure, Ferrari has been in the sport since William of Orange was running things but McLaren has just about the same number of Grand Prix victories. I fear that my basic problem with the F1 is that it was designed as a technological *tour de force* by someone using their head – not their heart. It obeyed the letter of the supercar law – but not its spirit. I admire it. But love it? No way.

2. FERRARI F50

Dealing with Ferrari is like trying to pick up mercury. Every promise they make is broken, routinely. If they say you can come to Italy to drive a new car, you know the trip will be wasted. There will be no car. So when they promised, after a two year barrage of requests, to let us drive a Formula One car I wasn't that excited. It would never happen. Not in a million years.

They also said we could drive the new F50 supercar, based on the Grand Prix car in question. And while there was more chance of this suggestion becoming reality, I still expected to meet Lord Lucan before it happened.

Nevertheless, we set off to Italy and there was the Grand Prix car glistening under a burning sun. They'd cut our filming time from two days to one. They'd invited some Italian journalists along, too. But they were going to let us play. And Tiff did just that for a whole, glorious morning.

Me? I went in search of the F50, which in the exalted company of a Grand Prix peregrine falcon, is like a common sparrow. And yes, it was there, too. But predictably, there was a problem. It had no plates and as a result I could not drive it outside the car park. I went mad. I explained in my best shouty English that we had invested a fortune in the story and that there was no point testing the Grand Prix car without the road car it had spawned. Tiff was out there risking his neck at 175 mph... and for nothing.

★BIZARRE *9. When a car crashed into a furniture shop window in Turin, witnesses said a man had wrenched open*

But they wouldn't budge, so I nicked it. Yup, when they weren't looking, I stole a £329,000, 202 mph supercar and headed off into the countryside. I'm told they were livid when they found what I'd done. They went more ballistic when they saw the resultant review on TV. You see, I didn't like it.

Leave aside the fact that this enormously expensive car has no carpets, radio or means of lowering the windows electrically. It needs to be light and these are small sacrifices if it means more speed. But it doesn't. It is still not that light. Indeed, the old F40 has a better power-to-weight ratio.

The F50 is not pretty, either. Like almost every Ferrari in history, it was penned by Pininfarina but, I suspect, while blindfolded and listening to white noise through headphones. Technologically, it was interesting. The front mounted fans both cool the engine and suck the nose onto the road, creating more downforce. There's the suspension which has no rubber components. Comfort? Pah. Driving this is like making love to a sack of bones. A supermodel, perhaps. At the back, the suspension is mounted to the gearbox which is nailed to the engine, which is nailed to the bulkhead where it forms a part of the chassis. But the engine itself is nothing special.

It was marketed as a direct development of the motor used by Alain Prost in his 1990 Grand Prix car, which has a certain ring. But in a rather fruitless quest for torque, it had been upped from 3.5 to 4.7 litres. And to keep the eco-weenies happy in places like Switzerland and California, its exhausts had to be stuffed full of very un-F1 things like catalytic converters.

The result was startling though. From 5,000 rpm upwards it went like a train to the accompaniment of a sensational sound. And the turn-in was incredible. There was no rubber in the suspension so there was no flex and consequently no delay. You turned the wheel and the car turned. Instantly. So well, in fact, that the back didn't stand a chance of staying in touch. Unless you were very careful, you'd become part of a fireball accident. This car redefines snap oversteer reminiscent of a Grand Prix racer.

I was terribly excited about the prospect of driving the F50 but it was too fast, too scary, too big and not good looking enough by half. And the police were waiting to have a chat when I got back.

SUPERMODEL EQUIVALENT
Someone young, bony and sexually underage. A night with her will get you into trouble.

he driver's door seconds before it collided. The man had then leapt from the car and run off down the street. An ▶

3. JAGUAR XJ220

The first time I drove a Jaguar XJ220, I was on a dead straight road that plunged through the heart of a desert in the United Arab Emirates. I knew then that it was indecently fast but also that it was too heavy. And that, basically, was that. But then, two years later, I found myself on a deserted stretch of sweeping A road in the middle of Wales and I simply fell in love with a car that's got more flaws than a 67 storey sky scraper.

First of all, it is huge, and I don't mean by that it was quite big, or even very big. I mean it was 17 feet long and nearly seven feet wide. I mean that it was bigger than a Diablo and therefore more striking than a hob nail boot applied with some force to the face. I have driven supercars all over the world and they all stop people in their tracks. But this one stops the sheep, the birds and the grass. I don't know about people – this was Wales, remember, and I didn't see any. Then there's the power. Now I know the XJ220 was supposed to have been equipped with a tweaked version of the Jag V12 and eventually came to the market with a twin turbocharged V6. But, frankly, I don't give a damn. It'll hold a McLaren all the way to 160, and eat a Ferrari F50 without even noticing.

What made all this especially scary was the location. This was not a desert, or a test track or Italy where speed is considered normal and

elderly woman found in the wreckage was taken to hospital with cuts, bruises and shock. Police traced the car's

important. This was Wales where there are corners and hump-backed bridges and errant sheep. And I was in a car that could get from rest to the speed limit in 3.8 seconds. Two seconds after that, it would be going past a hundred and one second later, I'd be on my way to hospital, via the windscreen. You see, the XJ220 has no brakes – not bad brakes, or inefficient brakes. But no brakes. You can stamp on the middle pedal with both feet and while the fearsome acceleration will stop, you'll be relying on friction to slow you down. This takes a while.

So, because you can't slow down for corners you learn pretty quickly about how much grip this car has. Maybe it's because of the weight or maybe it's because of that long flowing tail, but the back end of the XJ220 does feel glued to the road. Obviously, the mixture of a low gear with too much throttle will result in some sideways moments, but even then you can get it back on line with just the quickest dab of opposite lock. The XJ220 may be fast enough to bend time, but when the waywardness comes, it does so in surprising slow motion. And this means you don't get scared. And nor do you get thrown about in the leather-lined cabin either, because even my wife, who is officially a midget, has to drive along with her head wedged onto the roof lining and her knees jammed into the dash.

SUPERMODEL EQUIVALENT
Sophie Dahl: big, powerful, lots of things wrong; but striking.

Me? I have to practice the art of origami before I can climb inside. But it's worth it...or the fireworks. You see, when you need to manoeuvre Jag's biggest cat, the engine bay fills with smoke as the clutch burns – just one more reason for not having such a car. But then, of course, you get out there, put your foot down and everything becomes blurred. You can't see where you're going, which makes the point of this car crystal clear. Power.

owner, Primo Vitello, who told them: 'Yes, I jumped from the car. The woman is my mother-in-law. I had been ▶

4. FORD GT40

Funny company, Ford. Ever since the motor car's first few tentative steps, the blue oval has come to stand for nourishing home cooking. Ford is to the world of cars what the steak and kidney pie is to the world of cooking. But think about this. If you were forced to work in a kitchen making the same

driving her around the shops all afternoon and she kept complaining about my driving. Finally I could stand it no

MY TOP 20 DRIVES

THE CAR. . . . . . Ford Puma.
THE PLACE . . . . Bruntingthorpe Proving
Ground, Leicestershire.
THE DRIVER . . . Tiff Needell.
THE MEMORY . . We may mock Tiff for
being old and blind,
and for having lousy taste
in shirts, but when the
chips are down that boy
can really, really drive.
We were drifting at 100
mph in a car that, ten
minutes earlier, he had
never even seen before.

basic pie, day after day after interminable day, once in a while you'd want to make a lobster thermidore. Most of the time, of course, your boss will say, 'No, this is a roadside cafe, not the Ritz. Our job is to make pies.'

But just once, he'll say: 'Oh fooey. Go on then. Make me a lobster thermidore. And make damn sure it's better than any Italian dish you've ever tasted.' You see, in the early '60s Henry Ford had been on the verge of buying Ferrari, but at the very last minute Enzo pulled out of the deal fearful that his baby would be unable to survive under American ownership.

Ford was livid and decided if he couldn't buy Ferrari, he'd build a car which would beat and smash the Italians every time they stuck their head above the parapet. In America, engineers were told to develop an engine and gearbox combination which could be slotted into the middle of a chassis that was to be designed in Britain. The resultant mid-engined car

more so I told her to do it herself and leapt out.' ★BIZARRE★

MY TOP 20 DRIVES

THE CAR. . . . . . Jeep Wrangler.

THE PLACE . . . . Sierra Nevada Mountains, California.

THE DRIVER . . . Me.

THE MEMORY . . Scenery like I couldn't believe. The car was irrelevant. I mean, when Neil Armstrong played lunar golf, no one was terribly interested in what sort of clubs he was using.

was just 40 inches tall, hence its name – the Ford GT40.

The early lunges for racing glory were spectacularly useless, with the cars breaking down long before they had a chance to crash. And Enzo carried on, as troubled by the Ford effort as an elephant is by the presence of a house fly. But then came Le Mans in 1966. Ferrari, beset with industrial unrest at home, was not really firing on all twelve and despite a valiant effort from a private team in a 250LM, the 7.0 litre GT40 won the world's most famous race. And then in 1967, when Ferrari had no excuses, the Ford won again. And again in 1968. And again in 1969.

After this incredible run, the GT40 had a heritage to rival any other car on earth. Seeing the opportunity to claw back a few quid, Ford decided to make a road-going version with a boot. Unfortunately, the detuned, elongated version was rather watered-down and did not meet with much enthusiasm from contemporary journalists. So, after a production run of just seven cars, the plug was pulled.

I have never, as I'm sure you know, driven a Ford GT40, and I never will. I'm too big, by about nine inches. And too tall as well. But this, of course, is a good thing. All of us may hanker after some great car that was all the rage

★**BIZARRE** *10. Residents of a small village in Sicily were sceptical when a local magician announced his latest*

SUPERMODEL EQUIVALENT

Naomi Campbell. A supermodel from an unexpected source who's notoriously hard to work with.

when we were nine, but to be perfectly honest they're never as good as you think they'll be. Sure, an E Type looks great. But by modern day standards it's not that fast, it doesn't like corners and it's desperately uncomfortable and unreliable.

It hurts me to say this but the E Type is for poseurs. Keen drivers, and I'm not joking here, are better off with a Mazda MX5. The Ford GT40, I'm told, is a bit better in that it can do 165 mph and 0-60 in 5 seconds. So it is fast, and beautifully balanced, too. But I feel sure that the noise, the heat and the deep discomfort allied with comparatively uncommunicative steering and poor brakes would make it something of a nightmare in the real world. It's better then not to drive this car but to dream it.

and most daring trick – to drive his car around the town while blindfolded. The magician's first attempt was not a ▶

5. PORSCHE 911

If you were to walk up to a lion in the jungle and put your head in its mouth, you should not be even slightly surprised to emerge from the experience with no head. And yet if you were to capture the lion and train him, letting him get to know you bit by bit over a period of several years, you could put your head in his mouth safe in the knowledge that people will pay to watch. And so it goes with the Porsche 911. Designed originally for executives who'd had enough and wanted a quick and spectacular route to the next life, this was a car that would bite your head off and still want more. But Porsche has spent years training this vicious animal to behave, so that now you can plant your foot hard on the throttle half way round a wet corner and you'll simply go round the corner a little faster. Driving a Porsche 911

big success, as he crashed into a tree at the bottom of his driveway ten yards after setting off. However, he is

today is no more dangerous than pressing wild flowers.

I feel a little sorry for Porsche. You see, the old 911 was a flawed design. You cannot put a big heavy engine aft of the rear axle and expect the car to handle properly. Because it won't. By rights, it should have been quietly removed from production when the much better 928 came along in 1978. But by then, a select band of nutters had turned the 911 from a flawed car into a demi-god.

They would argue, noisily and with much finger pointing, that no car ever made could reward so graciously when the driver got it right. And they said it was only right and proper that it should bite so hard when the driver got it wrong. They said that all other cars on the market were muddle-headed and mediocre. They said that only the 911 truly understood the principle of the carrot and the stick. And we had to put up with all of this before they got to the engine which, of course, was air-cooled. Why was it air-cooled? If air cooling was such a brilliant idea, then why isn't every other car on the market air-cooled?

And off they'd go, waxing lyrical about the distinctive sound and the power and the torque blah blah blah. These guys would die for the 911. So, when the time came to think about perhaps replacing the 911 with something a bit more sensible, something a little more in tune with the times, Porsche's hands were tied. If they wanted to keep the 911 enthusiast happy, the new 911 had to be pretty much the same as the old 911.

My mate the Marquis of Blandford was first out of the blocks with a furrowed brow. Having owned and loved the old 911, he was nervous that the new one, with its softer lines, and traction control and water-cooled engine, would be an unleaded facsimile of the glorious original. He doesn't want to go round a corner, thinking that sophisticated electronics will get him out of trouble. He wants to go round the corner on his own. No way was he going to buy one of the new 911s. 'I'd rather have one of your Fiats,' he boomed, pointing at my Ferrari. But then we went for a drive in the new car. And though the interior has been re-arranged so that it now makes sense, he liked it. He loved the power, too, and the brakes, which are simply unbelievable. But most of all, he liked the fact that its engine is still in the boot. So he changed his mind and placed the order. And then it was my turn, and I set off gingerly expecting to feel its teeth biting into my neck at any time. But no.

optimistic about getting it right the second time. ★BIZARRE★

With 300 brake horsepower on tap, this car can get from 0-60 in 5.4 seconds and onwards to a top speed of 163 mph, making it nearly as fast as the 30-year-old GT40. But unlike the venerable Ford, this will stop and steer with the adroitness of a whippet. And it doesn't take very long before you're doing just that. Even with the traction control turned off, you just cannot make the back of this car slide at all. Too much speed on entry and it'll understeer. Too much throttle half way through the bend and it'll understeer. Lift off and it'll understeer.

And understeer is not even slightly scary to a child of the front wheel drive generation. I grew up with Golf GTis and I'm therefore used to it. I find it as natural as air. So pretty soon I was taking diabolical liberties, slamming the car into corners and stamping on whichever pedal most took my fancy. Lion? Pah. I've seen scarier geese.

Porsche's achievement really can't be overstated here because, with the new 911, they have a car that manages to keep the purists happy and bring in a whole new list of fans... like me, for instance. I've always been able to appreciate that a 911 can be

SUPERMODEL EQUIVALENT
Claudia Schiffer. German, sensible and old, now.

used every day, that it continues to be a supercar in the snow, ice and drizzle, that it'll keep going long after a Ferrari has shuddered to a halt. I've known, too, that it is well made and robust enough to provide owners with mile after mile of trouble-free motoring. And now, with the new car, those miles don't have to be quite so sweaty. I still don't think it provides you with the same level of fun as a Ferrari but then 'German' and 'fun' are not words which sit terribly well together.

However, it is now a car I respect enormously. ★

PLANET DAGENHAM

MR PRESCOTT'S PAGE

Which one of these Jags belongs to Mr Prescott? *Answer: Both of them*

Our idea of the perfect motoring holiday

Mr Prescott's perfect motoring holiday

Our dream car –.the Ferrari Daytona

Mr Prescott's dream car

85

SPORT

Obviously, the supreme car sport is motor racing, and much of what you will read in this chapter concerns itself with the greatest sporting spectacle of them all. I've looked at Formula One and how to improve it, the history of the British Touring Car Championship and why Le Mans gives you a headache. But cars have helped define other sports, too. When Reg Snozzer, the bent-nosed England striker, loses his licence for doing 130 mph past his old school, we have him clocked as the wild man of football. And when Ryan Giggs buys yet another Aston Martin, it's front page news in the *Sun*.

Car firms use sport to define image, too. When Audi launched the quattro, they started to sponsor horsey events, and it's no surprise to discover that Volvo sponsor golf.

'When I have conquered the world, I shall use the Berlin fire brigade to take Switzerland.'

SPORTS CARS

CRICKET

No one likes cricket. During a county match, you'll find more people in the church brass rubbing than you'll find on the hard wooden benches, watching a bunch of grown men taking it in turns to throw a rock at one another. The biggest problem with cricket is simple. It is so mind-numbingly dull that, simply to stay awake, the players have to take a break every afternoon for a caffeine injection. Sport is supposed to be fast paced and exciting, but cricket is as fast paced and as exciting as being dead.

If your team is fielding, you are forced to stand around all day trying to ward off hay fever until the opposing team's captain decides he's bored and calls it a day. Then you spend the next day sitting around in the pavilion waiting until someone decides its your turn to stand in front of three twigs that some bloke is trying to knock over with a bloody great rock. So, basically, cricket is all about man's ability to cope

★BIZARRE *11 Rottweiler Sam was definitely not man's best friend after driving off in his master's car. Sam's*

Eddie Irvine checks his stocks – the GTO needs its ashtray emptying.

with boredom... interspersed with periods of intense fear.

The perfect car, then, for people who choose this way of life is the Rover 400 diesel. Day after day, it moves you about offering absolutely nothing in return and then, one day, when you suddenly need a burst of acceleration to get out of harm's way... the diesel motor lets you down.

MOTOR RACING

In the top echelons of motor sport, the rules are very simple. Every day, a man comes to your house and shovels money through your letter box and then, once every fortnight – but only in the summer – you have to drive fast. In fact you drive so fast that ordinary road cars become ever so slightly dull. Michael Schumacher, who is a German, drives a Brabus Mercedes E Class estate which is listed in the *Guinness Book Of Records* as the fastest four door car in the world. Thanks to a 7.3 litre V12 motor, it can do 203 mph. And then there's Martin Brundle and Nigel Mansell, who have 500SLs. And Nelson Piquet and Alain Prost, who have 500SLs. Let's not forget, too, that Ayrton Senna had a 500SL. And that both David Coulthard and Mika Hakkinen have 500SLs – but as their race car has a Mercedes-funded engine, this is not surprising. Indeed, if you go down the grid asking each driver what he has in the garage at home, he will tell you

owner, Graham Stevenson, had left the handbrake off and the engine running as he popped indoors to pick up ▶

whatever his sponsors want him to tell you. But in reality, he will have a 500SL. All of them have 500SLs except Eddie Irvine, who has a Ferrari 288GTO – bastard.

So then, logically, this fanaticism for Mercedes makes sense. There's no point careering about in an inch-high supercar when you do that, and more, for a living. On the roads, surely you want something reasonably sprightly, but something which at the same time is comfortable, well made and available with a soft top hood. The tan is important. The tan makes you even more attractive to girls with dusky eyes and dental floss underwear.

You don't ever need to actually go anywhere in it – you have a helicopter and a private jet for that – you just use it for collecting milk and the Merc fits the bill perfectly. What really makes it better than the Jaguar XK8, though, or the BMW Z3, is simple. Mercedes offer Grand Prix drivers massive discounts.

MY TOP 20 DRIVES

THE CAR. . . . . . Range Rover Vogue SE.
THE PLACE . . . . The Empty Quarter, United Arab Emirates.
THE DRIVER . . . Me.
THE MEMORY . . There is a very large, very empty desert and there is the world's best off-road car... Now go and have some fun.

SNOOKER

To become good at snooker, you must spend your entire life in a darkened room, mixing with people who drink a vast amount of beer. I have never been able to finish a game because long before all the reds have gone, I'm so drunk that I can't even walk to the table. Once, I think, I scored a break of three but this can't be verified because my opponent was lying in a pool of his own vomit at the time. Or it may have been my vomit, I can't remember. In fact, now I come to think of it, I may not have scored three after all. It may have been one. Or none.

It's hard to think what sort of car should be driven by a snooker player and Stephen Hendry doesn't help. It seems that, over the years, he's had a

his wife. The fifteen stone dog immediately jumped in the car, nudging the automatic shift into 'Drive'. Witnesses

Rolls Royce, a Ferrari, a Mercedes, a Bentley and even a Skoda... which he won. I think, really, there's only one car that fits the bill — a Nissan Bluebird with a whippy aerial and a driver called Mr Patel from ABC Cabs. No snooker driver, surely, is ever sober enough to actually drive. And even if by some miracle they are, they should never attempt to do so during the hours of daylight. Because having been incarcerated for 20 years in a darkened room, they'd have to squint so much, they'd never see where they were going.

RUGBY UNION

A strange game, this. Basically you train – on a voluntary basis, usually – for years so that you can catch a ball while running at full tilt. You can dodge round oncoming players, and you can score drop goals time after time from anywhere within 50 miles of the posts. And then finally you run out onto the pitch where, for the next 80 minutes, you hit people in the face. Or rather, you would but it's hard when you're pinned to the ground by a bloke whose mother was a rhino and who's dad used to bite the wheels off low-flying aircraft.

Will Carling likes his Range Rover because it's handy for all that overnight luggage.

I played rugby once and couldn't believe it. For the entire duration of the match, people whom I used to call mates jumped up and down on my spine and, for afters, gouged my eyes out. Later, in the showers, they shaved all my pubic hair off and made me drink my own urine. Like I said – an odd sport. And there is only one car to have. Will Carling knows it and so, I guess, do all his mates. It's the Range Rover 4.6 HSE. Firstly, this is the only car big enough to handle a rugby player and, secondly, when the damn thing breaks down – and it will, a lot – rugby players are the only people on earth capable of carrying it home. Unless they're hungry of course, in which case they'll just eat it.

remember a car passing them with a dog's head and paws on the wheel. Sam safely avoided traffic coming the ▶

The Elise – plenty of room for a lunchbox.

ATHLETICS

Whenever it's athletics time and all four television channels show nothing but scrawny foreigners running around in circles, I do tend to reach for the paraquat. But I will admit that of all the sports and pastimes ever invented, the 100 metres sprint is by far the most pure. There is no luck involved and no rules to confuse the onlookers.

I should imagine therefore that the participants like things simple – food with no sauce, steroids but not in fancy bottles, holidays in Scarborough and cars without much in the way of bodywork. The Lotus Elise is perfect. It may not be the fastest, most powerful machine ever to stride onto the world stage but it comes out of the blocks like someone's just jammed a whole jar of chilli sauce up its backside.

GOLF

I think I see the appeal here. You get out in the fresh air but instead of simply walking round in a giant circle, which is pointless, you try to hit a ball into holes that have been carefully positioned along the route. Nice idea, really. Unfortunately, however, golf has been taken over by wankers who insist that you wear idiotic clothes and call everyone by their initials. Jeans are banned. The sharing of clubs is banned. Women are banned and if you walk through the east door when the chairman is buying

other way on the Surrey roads and managed almost half a mile with his owners running behind on foot. Mr a drink, you have to stand on your head and sing the theme tune to Thomas The Tank Engine.

Golf is a sport for people who are not simply small-minded but completely mind*less*. Learning the rules of the game is not that hard but learning the rules of the club can take forever. It is one of my lifelong ambitions to powerslide a Citroën Rallye Raid car across all 18 greens at St Andrews. Really, nothing would give me greater pleasure. Absolutely nothing – no, not even that.

Now, of course, I have been to a great many golf clubs and I have seen the car parks, which are full to bursting with Jaguars, Mercs and BMWs. But this is entirely wrong. If you wish to have a car that mirrors your appalling taste in clothes, it must be a Lexus. In the same way that the Golf Club Thought Police have taken a perfectly good concept and wrecked it with their dress codes and pettiness, Lexus have taken the perfectly good concept of executive motoring and added a slab of wood-look veneer. The Lexus may be more quiet, more reliable and better equipped than any of its European rivals, but it has no soul. It was built by a machine that follows the rules rather than a bloke in a brown store coat.

BOWLS

We're talking here about old people pottering down to the village to demonstrate that they can still bend slightly. And whenever you string the words 'old' and 'people' together, you are led inexorably to the next word in the chain which, invariably, is Honda. I'm thinking Civic here. I'm thinking beige. I'm thinking Roger Daltrey got it right and Robbie Williams had it all wrong.

'Easy there, left hand down a bit, mind the Civic's wing mirror.'

SKIING

If you've never done this, I can't stress the importance of doing so as soon as is humanly possible. To sit in an Alpine bar, sipping a glass of mulled wine as the sun beats down from an azure sky is one of life's greatest pleasures. I've been in Val d'Isere when the temperature has rocketed past 35 degrees – but

Stevenson finally managed to catch up, jump in and stop the car a few feet away from a brick wall. His wife Sue ▶

The Audi A8. All it needs is a roofrack.

it was August so the snow was a bit skimpy. Even in March though it can be t-shirt warm and then there are the views. To gaze out from your restaurant's balcony over mile after mile of snow-capped peaks is simply sensational.

Here's the weird bit, though. On holiday, I like to get up at about 10-ish, have breakfast, read the papers and just before lunch, gather up my skis and head for the hills. I'll gladly ski from wherever the chair lift stops to the nearest bar, but that's it until it's time to ski home again. What I do not understand are people who'll ski down the run and then want to do it all over again. And again.

These people haul themselves out of bed at 7 am, and apart from a brief lunch – which they merely treat like a refuelling stop – they ski ALL DAY, every day.

They say they want to get better at it... but why, when they live in Fulham for God's sake? They will

MY TOP 20 DRIVES

THE CAR. . . . . . **Mercedes 500SL.**
THE PLACE . . . . **Monte Carlo.**
THE DRIVER . . . **Mika Hakkinen.**
THE MEMORY . . **We may have been going slowly but being driven round the Monaco Grand Prix track by one of the nicest and most talented F1 boys was something special.**

said: 'Sam loves going in the car.' ★BIZARRE

never ever be a champion. To be really, really good you need to ski out of the womb. Only then will you have David Vine speaking your name in those hushed reverential tones. Only then will you look good in a Dayglo one-piece at 80 mph on the men's downhill.

But what sort of car should these guys drive? Well, as they have to live in the snow all day, it must have four-wheel drive but it cannot be a big and cumbersome off-roader. Some of me says the Subaru Impreza Turbo is right but it's a bit style free and skiing isn't. I'm therefore going to plump instead for the Audi A8 – but none of the versions that come equipped with sports suspension. If you have sports suspension on an Audi A8, your spine will shatter when you drive over as much as a pebble. And that buggers up your skiing good and proper.

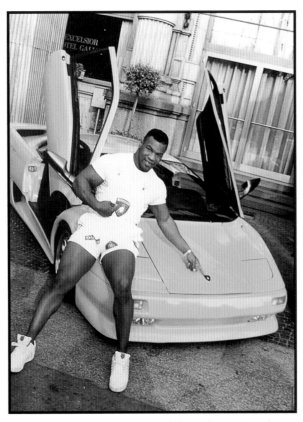

Mike Tyson helpfully points out where the badge on his shirt comes from.

RALLYING

You drive what the team bloody well gives you.

TOURING CAR RACING

If you woke up feeling a bit low this morning, don't worry. Maybe the cat was dead. Maybe there was a bill you just weren't expecting or perhaps you had a bit of tummy ache but honestly it could be worse. You could be Anthony Reid who, because he drives a Nissan Primera in the Championship, drives a Nissan Primera every day.

BOXING

Mike Tyson drives a Lamborghini Diablo. 'Nuff said.

WACKY RACES

or the participants, and especially their wallets, Formula One may indeed be the dog's conkers, but let's be honest, it can be a teeny bit tedious. How boring, exactly? Well, for a scale of dullness, let's start with an Open University programme in which a man with a beard explains why air is see-through. Below that comes a three-hour Hungarian subtitled film in which a man with another beard rediscovers his inner soul while restoring a cabinet. Then there's side two of Pink Floyd's *Ummagumma* and finally, on one of its bad days, comes a Formula One race.

The problem occurs when one team makes a huge technological leap and instead of drivers battling it out, the real race ends up being conducted thousands of miles from the track by Tefalheads in tyre laboratories. This is a grim state of affairs for you and I, the audience, but very good news for those repmobiles on drugs in the Touring Car Championship – easily the most consistently exciting track events in the world today. However, getting to the top has not been a basket of peaches and cream. Indeed, the sport has spent years, 40 of them in fact, trying to get itself sorted:

THE 1960s

The grid line-ups at the first Touring Car races looked like a bank robbers' convention, with row after row of Mk 2 Jags gunning their engines, blowing leaded fumes onto the ranks of *Italian Job* Minis lined up behind. The drivers, though, were quality chaps who seduced rather lovely popsies and spent several guineas an hour on Brylcreem. Then there were the young blades with names like Roy Salvadori, Graham Hill, Stirling Moss and Tommy Sopwith. The Formula One drivers would happily race Touring Cars because they had no problem running from car to car contesting four separate events at any one meeting. This way, they could pick up an extra two hundred and fifty quid for bashing the Jags round the track.

Since the series was designed – as it is now – to promote production cars on sale, only minor modifications were allowed. Roy Salvadori remembers that tyres could be swapped for racing tyres, but the actual size couldn't be altered. Likewise, engine modifications were Flintstone basic, such as shaving the cylinder heads to raise the compression ratio.

This delivered some utterly fantastic close racing and, because several classes raced at the same time, spectators were treated to some titanic David and Goliath duels between the Minis and the Jags. The Mk2s, particularly the 3.8s, had the horsepower and would bugger off when the sun shone, but on a wet day the lighter, faster-braking Minis would swarm among the big boys in the corners. Which would mean that much metal was banged and the skinny-tyred Minis were forever losing the plot and leaping over the barriers.

It was also fun. At one meeting the cars all started the race in reverse, but while this was great for the Woodbine puffing crowd, as ever in Britain, the class structure caused problems. I'm not talking about gentlemen's butlers attending to clutches in between serving the Pimms – that system worked very well – but rather the aggravation caused by different classes of cars competing in the same race.

Basically, a Jag driver who won the most races would not necessarily become the Touring Car champion for that season. If the bloke driving a poxy little Riley in the 'Up to 1600cc' class racked up more victories against other similar Moulinex-powered cars, then he would be the overall series winner, even though the big saloons would have crossed the finish line a fortnight in front of him. Indeed, the winner of the very first season drove an Austin Westminster, even though Tommy Sopwith — what a name! — in a Jag had won eight out of the ten races in his class. The system annoyed the drivers, but stayed in place until the current rule book was written.

On the bright side, this pick 'n' mix set up meant that the punters got to see a whole motor show on wheels. Star attractions for the mid 1960s were Jim Clark in his Lotus Cortina and then the big yank V8s – Mustangs, Camaros and Falcons. At first the Americans, with brakes made from old cowpats, were hopeless. But then Ford opened its wallet and the V8s ended the supremacy of the Jags.

THE 1970s

The first half of the decade saw the V8s battling, in much the same way the Minis had kicked the shins of the Jags, with the 2 litre Escorts. The five litre Americans could pump out 500 bhp against the tuned Escort's 290, which the medium sized Fords compensated for with shorter braking distances. But again, this back-and-forth struggle allowed the little people at the back to clean up: the overall Touring Car title for the first three seasons was won by a man driving a one litre Hillman Imp – until Frank Gardner's 7 litre Camaro finally did the business in 1973.

Dave Brodie in his Escort just before the After Eight moment.

And if life on the track was confusing, you should have seen what was going on behind closed doors in the garages. Nowadays, a modern motorsport scrutineer has to be capable of mending the gearbox on the Death Star, but back then they tended to be well meaning chaps in flat caps who tapped bits of the car with their pipes and nodded. The result was simple — the competitors indulged in some serious Boss Hoggery.

Andy Rouse, four times Touring Car champion, says it was a time when suspension points were laid out imaginatively, tyre sizes were here or

★**BIZARRE** *12. California Highway patrolman Edward Burt was suspended for one month without pay after a*

thereabouts and car bodyshells would be tipped upside down and dipped in acid to thin the top half and reduce weight. In a 1973 race at Silverstone, he recalls how Dave Brodie raced his Escort with a roll cage made out of hollow exhaust tubing and almost bought the farm when he got involved in a massive shunt which left his car shaped like an After Eight mint. Rule changes in the mid 1970s saw the American V8s outlawed for good and the 3 litre Capris took over as front runners in the big-engined class, winning five class championships on the trot.

The big new threat, though, came from the Japanese. Tom Walkinshaw entered Mazda RX7s which, with their light, powerful engines, cleaned up class championships for the next three seasons. Meanwhile, in the 1600cc category the Toyota Corollas smeared everyone else across the track, winning all of their 11 races in 1982.

THE 1980s

Frankly, with Toyota behaving like that, the racing was turning into the sort of spectacle only Ron Dennis would lock himself in the bathroom for. There was real action going on, but it was happening miles away from the track, in the High Court. In the 1980s, the 3.5 litre Rovers entered the fray, ending the dominance of the Capris, culminating in a clean sweep of the top three places in the 1983 season. Other teams immediately protested about Dick Dastardly behaviour regarding the mechanicals of the Rovers and investigations later proved that the rule book had indeed been used to balance a wobbly table leg somewhere in the canteen. Rover argued that the cars were legal, claiming they were homologated for some far off market like Kazakhstan-On-Sea, went to the High Court, then backed down and eventually disappeared, tail between exhaust pipes.

The second half of the decade was dominated by the turbo powered Sierra RS500s and the BMW M3s. Incredible cars, yes, but they made the racing as interesting as lettuce. One minute the Ford would chalk up nine out of 11 wins, the next the BMWs would snatch all the chequered flags, until it got to the point where BMW had racked up 27 victories on the trot.

Never let it be said the British rush into things. After more than 30 years of blokes tut-tutting about all the different classes of Touring Cars buggering up the racing, the penny dropped and everything that had gone before was swept away to make room for the present system: all engines

police investigation found him guilty of harassment. Long Beach resident Cathy Needham complained to Burt's ▶

had to be 2 litres, all had to run on unleaded, and there were specific weight parameters with tight controls about positioning the engine.

The decision was based partly on giving the crowds more exciting racing, but also because it made good business sense: every manufacturer has a 2 litre car in their line-up, which meant plenty of lucrative

When Sierra Man still voted Conservative.

work for the motorsport specialists. Ford was particularly keen on this move because the RS500s, which had only been eligible to race for five years, were coming to the end of their life and the Essex boys had nothing new in the pipeline.

While the Ford enjoyed a new career reversing into Dixons, everything went exactly as planned at the new Touring Car races. All the manufacturers brought their balls along and the 1991 season was tight, with BMW, Toyota and Vauxhall all winning enough races to bring on a climax the size of Meg Ryan's in *When Harry Met Sally*. Eventually the laurels went to Will Hoy in the BMW, and the following year was the most exciting of the lot, with the championship going right down to the wire in a pant-melting race at Silverstone, with Will Hoy, John Cleland and Tim Harvey all in with a chance of taking the crown and all of them, at some point in the race, being in a position to win. Tim Harvey won after his team mate, Steve Soper, removed Cleland from the action.

Drivers overtook (when one car passes another in a motor race), drivers crashed, drivers were watched by crowds which grew by the thousand. But it was never to be as good again. Scraps still take place throughout the field, but every year since, one manufacturer has cleaned up comprehensively – BMW, Alfa, Audi, Renault all walking away with it. Spoilers have popped up, too, which is great for joyriding but not much good when you want to see ten cars climbing into each others' gloveboxes as they come into a corner.

I, however, have thought of ways to make both TCC and F1 interesting...

superior officers about him continually pulling her over whenever he saw her car and the enquiry board ruled that

Nigel Mansell attempts, in his own inimitiable fashion, to make F1 exciting.

MY PLANS FOR FORMULA ONE

Formula One represents the very pinnacle of automobile endeavour and, as a result, car enthusiasts everywhere feel duty bound to be supportive. The fans would still turn up at the track, and the billions would still snuggle down in front of their TV every other Sunday, even if the drivers all went on strike. They've done it before, remember.

Yet I suspect this isn't really a sport we love. It isn't a sport we love to hate, either. It is, in fact, a sport we hate to love. We suspect it's all a big con when one McLaren pulls over to let the other one by, when Villeneuve allows people who have been helpful to overtake and when, in the

opping her 78 times in three months and issuing 43 traffic violation tickets was definitely harassment. The ▶

When F1 really was interesting – Hunt The Shunt leads the way.

nail-biting climax to a season, the top three drivers all qualify with exactly the same time – to within one thousandths of a second. Yet all these things are needed because this is a sport where pretty well every year, one team is utterly dominant and the racing, as a result, becomes pointless. You just give the prize to whoever happens to be employing Adrian Newey.

Actually, I use the word 'racing' carefully. For week after interminable week, these guys don't race. They don't dive up the inside in a do-or-die dash for death or glory. They don't drive the entire two hour Grand Prix at 10/10ths. They just follow each other round, which was fine in the days of ordinary gearboxes because from time to time a driver would screw up a change and the guy behind would nip by.

But today, there's no such thing as a missed change. You follow a guy at the start of a race and at the end the chances are you'll still be following him. And that heads up my five point plan for making Grand Prix racing More Interesting:

Point One: We ban the use of sequential gearboxes. And don't come crying to me, bleating about how F1 is supposed to be cutting edge because that's nonsense. Sure, some road cars do now use racing style gearboxes which, if you're very good, shave about a hundredth of a second of the meaningless 0 to 60 dash. This sounds like an awful lot of bother for very little gain. Believe me people, when I say that you don't need a clutchless gearchange.

Point Two. We allow teams to re-introduce ground-force cars. The current problem is that when you're up the gearbox of another car, he's messing with your aerodynamics so that just when you need to go faster than the guy in front, you end up going more slowly. And then you slide into a gravel trap. If the car was being sucked onto the road, you'd still have enough grip to skittle through on the inside.

Someone who can drive as well as Michael Schumacher (see point three).

Point Three. Find someone, somewhere, who can drive as well as Michael Schumacher. In fact, find 21 other people who can drive as well as Michael Schumacher.

Point Four. Give the coverage back to the BBC. I know I'm biased on this one, but unlike cricket where they change ends and break for tea, or football where they have half time, or tennis, where they have a lie down after every three games, there is no natural break in F1. And with no natural break, realistically, there's no space for a commercial break, either — let alone five.

Point Five. With these changes implemented, there will be no need for tiresome scheduled pit stops. Really, it's coming to something where the only excitement we get on a Sunday afternoon is watching a bunch of glorified Kwik-Fit fitters changing a wheel.

MY PLANS FOR MOTOR RACING

Right, that's F1 sorted out: now let's think up an entirely new racing formula to bring the sport forward a notch or two. Here are the rules:

1 Anything goes.

2 That's it.

You may turn up, if you wish, with a nitro boosted car that has eight wheels and a giant Hoover underneath. You may enter a hovercraft with four Merlin engines, or a radio-controlled mini car just four inches long.

Instead of feeding the same set of rules into the same sort of computer, as teams do now, this 'anything goes' philosophy would call for radical freefall thinking. It's this kind of lateral thought which really does pay dividends further down the line. If my new formula attracted the kind of sponsorship seen in Formula One, and therefore the sheer volumes of cash, they'd have cars running on tulips if they thought there was an extra horsepower or two in it. Indeed, I have *already* worked out how to win. I would turn up with a diesel powered car that does several hundred miles to the gallon but only 25 mph flat out. Doesn't sound like much of a winner, but it would be exactly the same width as the track. This would mean that I could never be lapped – and everyone else would overheat as they queued up in my wake.

All of them, eventually would need to pit and would rejoin the track behind me, not just on the track but for real. I'd win every weekend and it would become dull and predictable... just like Formula One.

Dammit. Back to the drawing board.

MY TOP 20 DRIVES

THE CAR . . . . . . Ferrari F50.

THE PLACE . . . . Dubai, United Arab Emirates.

THE DRIVER . . . Mohammed Bin Sulayem.

THE MEMORY . . If we get stopped by the police for doing this, nothing will happen.

F1 HALL OF FAME

GILLES VILLENEUVE

Countless racing drivers have been killed in action but I've singled out Gilles Villeneuve for two reasons. Firstly, he was the greatest racer ever to have lived and secondly, like Diana, he died because, some say, he wasn't wearing a seatbelt.

There was a time when Le Mans was very exciting.

A DAY IN THE LIFE OF LE MANS

t's June, 1957 – just before dawn and from away off in the distance, you can hear it coming – a finned and flamboyant Jaguar D Type. As it flashes past, you can see the driver, in a leather helmet and shirt sleeves, working the big wooden steering wheel. You note the grimace on his face as he slides that car on its unicycle wheels through the corner. And as the sun finally pokes its head above the Eastern horizon he's off, leaving nothing but the smell of Castrol R in his hazy wake.

This is the romance of Le Mans. It was a gentleman's event which provided an excuse for other gentlemen to drive their gentlemanly cars to Northern France every Summer. Where, after watching the race for a couple of hours, they'd head into town for dinner and afterwards, the luxury of Egyptian cotton sheets in an agreeable *auberge*. Six hours later, after some

★BIZARRE *13. An Australian motorist charged with public indecency while driving naked pleaded innocent, on*

sleep and a foaming bath, they'd be back at the track for a day's racing and some Pimms.

Now, spool forward 40 years to 1998 and you'll find that, while the race is still going, it's become about as romantic as a survey into public transport needs for the 21st century. Today, only the *tales* of derring do remain: There was a chap who pulled into the pits as night fell so that he could change into evening wear. And there was one team who, after being told they couldn't race, went into town and drank it dry. Then, an hour before the race began, they discovered there was a slot after all. Now these guys were drunk – really badly wobbly – and yet they went out there... and won. Marvellous times.

But not any more. First of all, every single one of the drivers these days – even Tiff Needell – is stone cold sober. And they wear overalls, not dinner jackets. And even in the open cars, you can't see them working the wheel or the expression on their faces, because they're entombed in full metal crash hats, with tinted, perspex fixtures.

And what of the cars? Back in the 1950s and 1960s, the drivers would actually drive their race cars to Le Mans, race them and drive them home again. But not any more. Sure, the rules say they must race cars that are made for the road but they just aren't. That Nissan R390 has about as much to do with the Almera as cheese. And the same goes for the Lister, the BMW, the Mercedes, the Porsche and the Toyota. They. are. not. road. cars. Got that?

And yet still, every year, the Eurotunnel and the ferries fill to the point where even a veal would complain as British fans head over to France. I don't get it. Unless you're very lucky, or very organised or prepared to travel a very great distance, you aren't going to find an agreeable French *auberge* in which to stay. So you can forget all about Egyptian cotton sheets and piping hot coffee in the morning.

You're going to get to the track – on a coach, most likely – and you will not leave it again until the race is over. Actually, the traffic will be so bad at this point, you won't leave it then, either. And boy, will you be knackered. You see, upon arrival at, say, lunchtime on the Saturday, you'll have had a brief look round, note that your tickets only entitle you to the lavatories, and that as a result you're not going to get within 100 yards of the Hawaiian Trop Girls. You will therefore have suggested to your mates that you should

account of his girlfriend's head covering his lap at the time. Twenty-three-year-old Richard Cooper argued that ▶

His insistence on waving to Eva meant Adolf never won at Le Mans.

hit the beer tent where, under a fearsome sun, you'll sit for three hours. You'll miss the start because after three hours of drinking under a fearsome sun, all anyone wants is three more hours of drinking. But after six hours of drinking, all anyone wants is a bed with Egyptian cotton sheets, and as I've already explained, that isn't possible. So instead, you head for the fairground where you stagger about, staring at naked women who are fat, and queuing for a ride on the dodgems. By this stage, you are a broken spectacle who can think of nothing but getting your head down somewhere – but you can't because the coach is locked, and there's an interminable din coming from the track. Won't those bloody cars ever shut up? No, they don't. So you wobble about some more before, at 4am, having lost all your mates, you collapse in a heap round the back of the public lavatories – the French public lavatories.

One hour later, it starts to get light and, with the hangover from hell, you begin to stir. Now, this is not a headache, as such. This is a tornado that's tearing up your soul. There is a hurricane in your guts and a lightning bolt in your cranium. Plus, it feels like someone has defecated in your mouth which, as you've been sleeping by the lavatories, is a very real possibility.

You lurch off in search of coffee and after three cups, you start to feel a

with his girlfriend's head there, his private parts were covered. Magistrates agreed and let him off. ★BIZARRE★

108

little better. And you've found your mates, one of whom suggests a hair of the dog or *cheveaux du chien*, as they say over there. So at about seven, you start on the beer again until by ten, you are not drunk, or even pissed. You are insane. You are so insane that you think it would be a good idea to watch some racing. So, arm in arm you wander off in search of the track where, for the first time, you see – rather than hear – some racing cars. Neeeeeeow!, they go at ten second intervals. It takes about a minute to realise that, actually, they all look pretty much the same and about another ten minutes to work out that you haven't a clue who's winning. So you turn to the spotty boy behind who has his ear clasped to a transistor radio, listening to coverage of the race on Radio Le Mans. Enthusiastically, he says that Fabruzzio is in the lead by eight laps – laps, not seconds – from D'Arcy who is fourteen laps clear of Wonkleburger Jnr. You've never heard of any of them. And through your beer goggles, you can't tell which car is what either.

You pass out where you lie in what is technically a coma until the race finishes and a Porsche of one sort or another has won. Only this time, when you wake up, you really are in a bad way. You have eyes like ordnance survey maps and vocal chords that just make squeaking noises. When you try to talk, you sound like a rabbit. You have sunburn. All there is between you and home are six hours on a coach getting out of the car park, six hours to Calais, two hours sick on a boat and three hours on a coach in England.

But next year, you'll be back for more. ⭐

MY TOP 20 DRIVES

THE CAR . . . . . . Ford Mustang 5.0 litre drop head.

THE PLACE . . . . Silverstone, Northamptonshire.

THE DRIVER . . . Michael Schumacher.

THE MEMORY . . He may have been the most monosyllabic, arrogant and rude bastard I've ever had the misfortune to meet, but his driving was sublime. He could even make a Mustang sit up and beg.

Keith Moon in his normal driving outfit; he should have taken up motorsport.

MOTORSPORT BAD BOYS

Excitement for a modern Formula One driver means having the little swirly bits of pasta instead of the long straight stuff. But a few years ago, they were giving Keith Moon a run for his money:

★ **America 1962;** Innes Ireland, out in the States to race sports cars, had been wearing his drinking trousers all day. In the evening, he and his mates, equally blathered, got onto that great philosophical discussion: do headlights work under water? Innes settled the matter by driving his hire car into the swimming pool.

★ **Paris 1956;** Two days before the Monaco Grand Prix. Mike Hawthorn broke his journey down to the Riviera with a stopover in the French capital.

Several tons of beer later, he was on the rampage in a French brothel, running into bedrooms and pulling customers off the other women to see if he can find a better hooker than the one he's got.

Hawthorn's best mate, Peter Collins, could be equally mischievous. On a cross channel ferry bound for a race on the continent, he was bored to death by an American who droned on about the supremacy of American cars and their huge V8s over the miserable British automotive offerings. Collins said nothing but politely asked the American to show him his car down in the hold, and the American thought nothing of it until the time came to disembark. Collins asked the offending Yank to put his foot down and demonstrate the power of the V8, forgetting to tell him that he'd chained the car's back axle to a pipe on the boat...

★ **The Grand Prix at Rheims;** always a favourite with the teams during the 1950s, on account of the vats of champagne on offer. The day would perhaps start with Graham Hill and Innes Ireland carting another driver's bubble car upstairs and putting it outside his room on the landing, then American driver Dan Gurney would blow up a few toilet cisterns with his homemade bombs. Invariably, come the evening, the French plod would arrive to sort out the pissed up drivers. 'The trick then,' recalls Roy Salvadori, 'was to keep them talking while some of us went outside to put their van on bricks.'

★ **London 1966;** Graham Hill was at a swanky dinner when a stripper was brought on. Having enjoyed a sherbet, Hill decided to help the gal disrobe. However, to reach her, he had to run across some tables. Halfway there, one collapsed and he fell onto a wine glass stem which gouged straight into his knee. 'Fortunately,' said Hill, 'I was in my underpants at the time or else I would have ruined my trousers.'

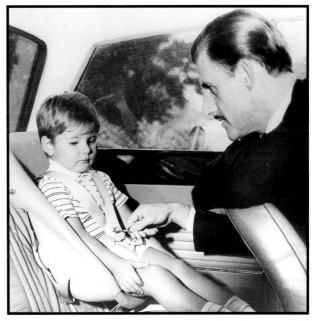

'Now listen, Damon, when I'm in the front seat I do the driving, right?'

'Hell-oh!' James spies the prey.

★ **Around the world, 1970s;** James Hunt was one of the few who carried the torch into the late 1970s and was a regular passenger onboard the good ship Tomfoolery. At the Canadian Grand Prix during his championship winning 1976 season, Hunt arrived for a test session but instead was distracted by a girlfriend of one of the marshalls. Launching into full Leslie Phillips mode, he quickly lured her into an ambulance parked nearby. Hunt's mechanics engaged her unsuspecting boyfriend in conversation while the ambulance rocked merrily away in the background.

A couple of years back Gerhard Berger recounted a little gem about Nelson Piquet, from the days when he was driving for Bernie Ecclestone at Brabham. It seems that Nelson had been dipping his wick at two separate addresses, and lo and behold, when he came off the track into the pits during qualifying, both girls were standing there, oblivious of each other, waiting to talk to him. Ever the gentleman, Nelson floored it back out of the pits, leaving team boss Bernie screaming at him to come back in and stop wasting precious qualifying laps. Piquet refused to return until the chick situation had been sorted out. ★

GRAND PRIX SPECTATOR

She's called Debbie-Ann and she has never been to a motor race before. She thinks she may meet a driver – Jean Alesi, she hopes – which is why she is wearing that dress and those shoes. She is only going because her husband – Dave – is the photocopier salesman of the month and has won the tickets. Over lunch she will drink too much free pomagne and will fall asleep. She will awake half way though the race with a splitting headache and then moan for the rest of the day. She will not meet Jean Alesi. She is the reason why you couldn't get a ticket – and even if you could, why that ticket would cost you about £900 million. ⭐

A Citroën Rallye Raid being driven by an expert.

RALLYE RAID

Driving a racing car is like camping. You could stay in a nice bed and breakfast somewhere with sheets and central heating but oh no, you've got to get out there, in the countryside, under canvas, with no lavatories for 40 miles. I've never really seen the point but I'm told that, when camping, you feel at one with the earth and I suppose you do. I did it in Australia recently and very nearly became a part of the earth. Every 15 minutes, I'd wake to find another poisonous snake or spiky insect was tucking in its napkin while eyeing up my soft white underbelly. And so it goes with racing cars. You could buy an ordinary saloon with velour trim, a wood-look dash, soundproofing and electric windows. It would be nice, quiet, and comfy.

Or you could invest instead in what basically amounts to a shell and an engine. The sound of that motor reverberating around a metal box has to be heard to be believed... and then there's the suspension. Or rather, there isn't. You may have driven a Corvette, which is very probably the

★**BIZARRE** *14. Delivery driver Sean McDowell, from Wexford, Eire, was pulled over by traffic police while doing*

firmest riding road car ever, but it is a marshmallow compared to even the most simple racer.

Racing cars are distressingly uncomfortable – and hot – but without any of life's little luxuries you are left with a certain purity, a certain one-ness with the thrill of driving. You see, a race car doesn't need to last thousands of miles or be quiet. It needs to be fast. And that's it.

Over the years, I've driven a great many, from rally cars to touring cars and from single seaters to swamp buggies and all of them are deeply unpleasant. The basic problem is this: they brake more efficiently than you think possible so you end up hitting the middle pedal where you think it's prudent only to find you've ground to a halt some 300 yards before the turn starts. It takes a day or so to work out that the car will stop if you so much as blow on the brake pedal and then you can start to experiment with cornering speeds. Now, I can look at a curve and have a pretty good idea how fast I can get round it. In an ordinary road car, this mentally-noted speed is probably within 95 per cent of the car's ability, but in a race car it's only ever about 50 per cent

If you have slick tyres, you don't need a brain. You just get to any corner, at any speed, turn the wheel and you'll sail round. Seriously, I've never even been close to a race car's limits. Not even when I found myself in a Maestro club racer. Not even in a Skoda rally car. Never. This, though, is a good thing. You see, in a road car you know when all hell is about to break loose because the car is leaning violently on its soft suspension, the tyres are squealing and it's all feeling very nervous.

But in a race car, I'm told, everything feels absolutely fine... until all of a sudden, it isn't. One minute you're heading east, and the next you're still heading east... only backwards. That's what separates racers from lesser mortals – they can recognise the moment when it's about to go wrong and react accordingly. We just crash. Frankly, it's all a bit disheartening. When you've psyched yourself up to take a bend at a speed you consider to be suicidal, only to find that you are exiting the bend on the inside with 30 yards of track to spare, you know you will never make the grade in automotive competition.

However, there was one race car I drove – a fully-fledged works prepared machine – that I simply loved. The Citroën ZX Rallye Raid. It's small and hot inside a car like this. And so scary that you tend to find

3 mph. The speed was not the problem. Police were more concerned that Sean had been driving along the ▶

A Citroën Rallye Raid being driven by Clarkson. A World Champion was scared. Really.

yourself laughing like an idiot, rather than screaming. To start with, Timo Salonen was in the driver's seat and he wasn't talking – which is always a bad sign. When you're out with a race driver and they are chatting away, you know they aren't going very fast. If they are silent, it's because they are concentrating, absolutely, on not killing themselves.

Which means it has crossed their minds that they *could* kill themselves. Which means they are going as fast as they can. Now, please bear in mind at this point that Timo Salonen is an ex-world rally champion and that he was at the wheel of a full-blown, ultra-competitive rally car which had been specially built for events like the Paris-Dakar – thousand mile races across the desert. It is a huge, high-riding, four-wheel drive, turbocharged monster that spits flame when you change gear and tries to kill you. And then, with me still laughing like a man whose daughter's life depended on it, Timo brought the car to a halt and said it was my turn to drive.

We were in the South of France, on a special piece of rock- strewn track designed to resemble the Sahara. There were crests and switchbacks and

motorway playing his flute with both hands, and steering with his feet. 'He only put the flute down to turn off the

MY TOP 20 DRIVES

THE CAR . . . . . . Mahindra Jeep.
THE PLACE . . . . the Bombay to Pune
road, India.
THE DRIVER . . . Me.
THE MEMORY . . In a country whose
roads kill **168** people
every day, we lived.

ridiculous hills and dips. Well I think there were but it's hard to be sure because the dust kicked up by Timo's driving was still out there, lingering like the sort of strange mist they have in pre-war horror films.

Nevertheless, I bravely squeezed my bum into a seat that had been designed for Kate Moss, wedged my balls into the 5 point harness, fired up the mid mounted engine and let rip. Now, obviously, I was expecting to find myself stopping 500 yards before every bend, which I would then crawl round at quarter speed. But no. On the very first turn, I squeezed the throttle open at the apex and the back started to slide. It was a lovely, slow, graceful drift, too, that wasn't even the slightest bit scary so I simply applied some opposite lock and kept my foot hard in it. The car straightened and rocketed itself to the next bend, where the same thing happened.

By this stage, I was starting to increase my entry speeds a little and found I'd be diving into the turns with understeer — something that was easily corrected with more power. So then I started flicking it into corners, to kick the back out before the turn began and that worked, too. It seems that to cope with the rough surface, the Citroën has soft suspension which makes it handle more like a road car. But I don't care *how* it was happening. I was just dribbling with excitement that it was happening at all. After five laps, I was going fast enough for Timo to ask if he could get out and never, not once in my whole miserable life, have I ever felt so happy. I had scared a world champion rally driver out of the car. Usually, when I'm driving, they just fall asleep.

Now I know that desert raid rallying is a sport for old men and that the cars are comfortable on their long travel springs. But I don't care. It was a works rally car that even I could drive properly. ⭐

motorway,' said the officer in court. McDowell, banned for one year and fined £250, said he preferred listening ▶

117

Ryan Giggs and his Aston Martin. Smart lad.

FOOTBALLERS & THEIR CARS

There is one fundamental difference between the old rich and the new rich. The old rich use their money to buy *time*. I know of one aristocrat who is prepared to spend an entire afternoon trying to guess whether the butler used a steel or silver knife to cut the crusts from his cucumber sandwiches. The new rich use their money to buy *things* – holidays, indoor swimming pools, snooker tables, clothes and, most of all, cars.

The old rich, having been brought up with money, see no reason to shout about it and consequently buy cars for purely practical purposes. I could show you to the door of a man who owns most of a Midlands county but he drives round in a beige Renault estate – well, what's left of it,

to live music rather than tapes or the radio. ★ BIZARRE

anyway. The dog has already eaten most of the passenger seat and all of the gear lever. This doesn't matter. The old rich have enough money to buy a new car when the dog finally gets round to the engine but it will still be a dull-coloured Subaru or a navy blue Golf with steel wheels. Anything, really, that doesn't attract attention.

Now let's move to the neo-Georgian suburbs of town, where the driveways are full of BMWs and Mercs. Here, the car is not a tool; it's the best way of advertising your wealth. Drive into town in a new Range Rover and no one is left in any doubt. You have a lot of money, and with the fuel injectors squirting fuel into the eight cylinders at the rate of one gallon every ten miles or so, everyone is aware that there's plenty more coming in next week's pay cheque.

And who best typify the new rich? Well obviously, you'll find a fair few whenever the Lodge is meeting, and golf club car parks are a fine hunting ground, too. But I think the answer, really, is professional sportsmen, or to be specific, professional, Premier League footballers. Football trawls the backwater housing estates for talent. No footballer was born with a silver spoon in his mouth. They tend to be educated so badly that most are incapable of coherent speech and yet, if they are able to kick an inflated sheep's pancreas accurately, a man in a sheepskin coat will give them £20,000 a week – maybe more. Now, these guys are young and not very clever, so instead of putting some aside for when the knee injury comes calling, they splash out on bullseye glass conservatories, designer underpants and, top of the list – cars. Ryan Giggs, Ian Wright, David Platt and Dwight York have all, at one time or another, owned an Aston Martin DB7 and, really, it's not hard to see why. Quite apart from the fact it is — no arguments please – the best-looking car ever made, it is also a supercar that you can use every day.

If you're going to show people just how much money is at your disposal, there's no point buying a piece of exotica that has to stay in the garage whenever it's foggy, windy, cold, hot or wet. You need something that's out there all the time and, quite frankly, you can't do much better than a DB7. It is, after all, the car that James Bond would be driving had BMW not paid him £4.50 to use a 750. Obviously, the faster Jaguar XK8 is a more sensible buy but we're talking here about a bunch of guys in their early 20s. Sensible is just another word for corduroy. They want – need – to be able to

David Beckham and his bit of Posh. Victoria's in there, too.

tell people that they have an Aston and that it's outside right now.

When it comes to year-round high-speed appeal, the Aston Martin only has one serious rival – the Porsche 911, and a little research shows that this too finds favour in round ball circles. David Beckham, Nicky Butt, Les Ferdinand, David Seaman and Neil Ruddock are fans of the arse-engined Nazi staff car. Strangely though, Jason McAteer has a Porsche Boxster. Well, it's strange until you think things through here. You see, the only reason for being fit, young and rich is to have sex with as many girls as possible. Now, let's say the Liverpool boys are out on the town together, grooving their stuff in Shitters nightclub or wherever. The girls are interested but which one is it to be – they're all fit, young and rich – and they all have 911s, which are men's cars.

Tell a man you drive a 911 and he'll stand back and gawp in admiration. You are brave and talented, able to handle whatever the laws of physics send your way. Men know that the 911 can be a tricky little bastard. Women, however, tend not to be quite so clued-up. In girldom, the 911 is just noisy, cramped and ugly. The Boxster, on the other hand, is quite the coolest car around. We know it's dog slow. They don't. By driving such a car, Mr

McAteer has an edge. While his team mates can get home more quickly, Jason goes home with someone else – and that's what matters.

Which brings me neatly onto Mercedes Benz – or, in footballer speak, home. The greatest thing about Mercedes is that you can start off, when young, with an SL which, to quote *Viz*, is not so much a car as a fanny magnet. They're wrong, actually. It is THE fanny magnet. Some say oysters

The Porsche Boxster; car of choice for the footballer who wants to pull.

are an aphrodisiac but gargling on salty snot is no match for the two-seater Teuton drop top. And when your playing career is over and the dug-out beckons, you need something a little more spacious, something that can accommodate your new found gut and the *de rigeur* sheepskin coat – Mercedes have a vast range on offer.

There's the new four wheel drive M Class, there's the E Class estate or, for the chairman, the S Class continent crusher. It's no surprise to find that both Alex Ferguson and Terry Venables are committed to the three-pointed star. All football managers are. If you go back into the origins of the Spanish language, you'll probably find that Mercedes actually means, 'Someone who wears a sheepskin coat and has a fondness for shouting.' And there's more. After the inevitable row with the directors, it's time to start up a bar somewhere with live boxing. The days of big cash are over, but still Mercedes is there to help out with its range of E Class diesels and the C Class, which is a dog in more ways than one. A Mercedes is not just for Christmas – it's for life.

Now there are exceptions to the rule here. Gary Lineker, the man with the neat haircut who has never said 'bugger' in his whole angelic life, drives a Lexus. Of course he does. And so does John Barnes. And so does Howard Wilkinson, who was a manager but is now technical director to the Football Association. Sounds interesting.

Then you've got sponsorship deals which puts Gazza in a Honda Accord,

The goalscorer's choice: A Jag XKR. Perfect for posing in, as well as driving very fast.

Steve McManaman in a sick coloured Nissan Primera and Alan Shearer in a Jaguar XK8 – spawny git. The entire Aston Villa team has to potter about in a selection of Rovers. Chrysler seem to have sunk their claws into the ,too, with Nicky Butt, Andy Cole, Lee Dixon and Trevor Sinclair all having Grand Cherokee Jeeps. Some even have Voyager people carriers.

An odd choice, that, until you begin to work it out. If you drive around in something with seven seats, people assume you have a great many children and that, therefore, you're nothing more than a big sack of testosterone. These things aren't cars at all – they are, as AA Gill put it in *The Sunday Times*, breeder wagons.

So what of Ferrari? Why do we not the see the greatest name of them all cropping up, time and again, in footballdom? Well, first of all, you can't use a Ferrari every day because it's somehow too precious. You can't leave it parked outside a nightclub in Burnley because when you come out it will have been turned into a DeLorean. And each time it goes for a service, they have to take the engine out. And the clutch is heavy, and the sound system is pitiful. Obviously, some footballers have gone down the Ferrari route but it's never a long lasting love affair – Alan Wright sold his because the driving position hurt his knee – diddums. The *nouveau riche*, you see, like wipe-down fabrics and microwaved food. They like remote-control bath water and hot and cold running satellite television. They believe that life can, and should, be conducted from the comfort of a Dralon Parker Knoll recliner and, quite frankly, a Ferrari is too much like hard work.

Indeed, I've trawled the lists and can find only two players who bought Ferraris and are sticking with them – Manchester United's Teddy Sherringham, who has a 355 Spider and Spurs' Les Ferdinand, who has a 550 Maranello. Chaps, you're welcome round at my house any time.

★BIZARRE *15. When Brazilian paint salesman Carmeto Silva was flagged down twice within the hour by the same*

Dagenham Alf's 1970 World Cup Squad and their sponsor's fleet of Cortinas.

BACK THEN

Today, a football player can pay cash for an XK8 out of his earnings from a Wednesday morning training session. Score a goal or two on Saturday and Maranello is your oyster.

However, in 1966, when we sent the Hun packing for a third time, things were a little different. On the Wembley pitch, British fans witnessed our finest football moment to date but despite their dribbling skills, Bobby and Nobby were not exactly over-endowed in the garage department. My line-up overleaf shows that England's greatest ever team was, from a vehicular point of view, on a par with the bloke who pushed the roller across the pitch. Hardly surprising, really, since their wages were around £100 per week, and for winning the World Cup they each trousered the princely bonus of £650.

Come the 1970 World Cup, though, Ford hurled itself on the publicity bandwagon and doled out a free 1600E to each squad member in the

traffic cop, he decided enough was enough and leapt from his van to pour a tin of red paint over the policeman. ▶

Peter Osgood shows why Chelsea were always the team for the fashion-conscious.

defending champions' line up. As Jack Charlton remembers it, the players could keep them for a whole year and then have the option to buy them. Obviously reeling in shock from the car giant's boundless generosity, the team went and lost the World Cup. In 1974, we didn't even qualify, but by then it didn't matter: footballers had sussed they could get more out of the game than free Brylcreem and long shorts. Kevin Keegan would soon be flogging Harry Fenton threads and George Best was saying: 'On second thoughts, make it a double.' The only people, in fact, enjoying life more than the footballers were their local car dealers. There's a moral in here somewhere about money and fame, but it'll be dull, so I won't bother. ⭐

In court, the traffic cop said he had only flagged Silva down a second time to tell him that the earlier booking he

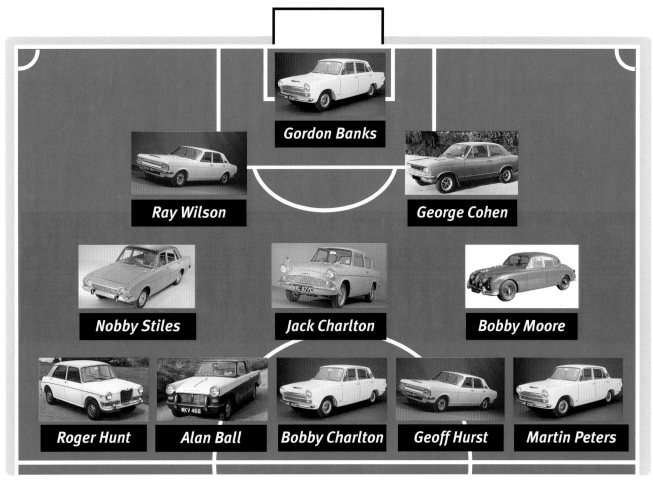

Gordon Banks

Ray Wilson
George Cohen

Nobby Stiles
Jack Charlton
Bobby Moore

Roger Hunt
Alan Ball
Bobby Charlton
Geoff Hurst
Martin Peters

1. Gordon Banks Ford Cortina; 'Can't remember much about it. I think the back lights were all in a circle.' Right. **2. Ray Wilson** Ford Zephyr. **3. George Cohen** Vauxhall Viva with a Brabham conversion. Unlike Gordon Banks, George was the car enthusiast of the side. The Brabham-converted Vauxhall featured lowered suspension and a straight through exhaust. George got the car for a discount by doing an advert in the Surrey Comet for Jack Brabham's dealership. **4. Nobby Styles** Ford Corsair. **5. Jack Charlton** Ford Anglia. **6. Bobby Moore** Unfortunately Bobby has gone on to that great sub's bench in the sky, but his team mates seem to remember him driving a Mk 2 Jag. **7. Roger Hunt** Riley Kestrel. This was the Escort Ghia of its day, a slightly upmarket Austin 1100 with wood and leather. Roger's was a pleasant beige. **8. Alan Ball** Triumph Herald. **9. Bobby Charlton** Ford Cortina. **10. Geoff Hurst** Ford Zephyr. **11. Martin Peters** Ford Cortina.

had dished out for speeding was a mistake. ★BIZARRE

PLANET DAGENHAM

TV

'd like to bet that every single man over the age of 35 out there can't remember a single plot line from *The Persuaders* – a televisual detective feast starring Tony Curtis and Roger Moore. But every single one of them knows exactly what sort of cars they drove. The Car really is the Star and never is this more true than in 1960s and 1970s television, when we had *The Saint* in his Volvo and Jack Regan in his Granada. See the car. Know the man. Know the man. Buy the car. At the height of Arthur Daley's popularity, sales of second-hand Jags went through the roof. You almost never see an advertisement for Jaguar on TV. With Morse and Arfur out there, they don't need to bother. Reliant should have tried, though. Before Del Boy came along, their Robin van was a sensible and cheap means of getting your business off the ground. Not any more. TV killed it.

TOP GEAR ON TV

"Suave, handsome, a man of independent means, lives in a mews house in Mayfair, drives a... "

This last detail was where the TV script-writers of the 1960s and 1970s would stop pounding the typewriter, light a fag and reach for the *Observer Book Of Cars*. Anything would do as long as the chosen wheels were interesting and sporty. After all, here was the writer's one chance to make his hero different: *The Saint*, *The Baron*, *The Persuaders*, *The Avengers*, *Department S*: the heroes all used Brylcreem, all shared the same post code, all had no visible means of paying the gas bill, but the car could be a Volvo, a vintage Bentley or a Jensen.

A perky automobile was also a cheap way of adding colour to TV programmes that were, let's face it, complete crap. Those 'action' series were like wedding cake — promising to look at but with contents tasting of old peoples' pants. They had dismal plots, shabby action and no budgets – whenever *The Saint* rocked up in a foreign dictatorship he was inevitably in

★BIZARRE *16. Jealous husband Stefano Bendi tried to catch his wife Genia with her lover by hiding in the boot of*

North London, surrounded by the props from the last *Carry On* film. It's almost a rule that the worse the series, the better the car was. *The Baron* is a classic example. Here we were promised a generously side-parted Steve Forrest playing a dashing antique dealer who gets himself caught up in nail-biting adventures on a weekly basis. What we got, in reality, was a man who sells occasional tables hitting a foreigner in a Fez at the end of every episode. And when I say 'hit', I don't mean some Hollywood **KERRUNCH** , but a polite Elstree biff. It was up to the car parked outside the mews house to save the day, and indeed there it was, a truly charismatic and competent Jensen CV8 with a massive 6.3 litre Chrysler V8.

Department S was equally hopeless, a sanctuary for lines such as: 'You're going to prison for a very long time.' The main action hero, a coiffured and cravated Jason King, looked about as convincing as Liberace in a welding shop, but butchness was thrust upon him in the shape of a Bentley Continental (opposite).

John Steed of *The Avengers* also opted for a Bentley to ferry him between bomb defusings and cellars where circular saws needed switching off. It was, it has to be said, a truly impressive-looking 1920s 3 litre, but why drive some thirsty old vintage chugger when you're so busy? Some time into the run of *The Avengers*, the production company tried to put Steed in a much faster AC Cobra, but Patrick MacNee personally vetoed the idea, ensuring that his character continued to arrive in the nick of, rather than plenty of, time.

Steed's (second) sidekick Emma Peel displayed a tad more crimefighting common sense by driving a Lotus Elan which mysteriously changed from white to blue during the run of the series. Legend has it that the model changeover was not exactly planned by the TV people: apparently, one of the Lotus employees had a big argument with Lotus boss Colin Chapman and drove off in the white Elan – Emma Peel's white Elan – never to be seen again.

The other significant righter of wrongs around this time was Simon Templar, a.k.a. *The Saint*. Again, much the same formula as *The Baron*: tourist board shots of Piccadilly Circus, guns that no one fired and baddies with cigarette holders saying: 'Find the girl/diamonds/microfilm before Templar gets to her/them/it.' In the Roger Moore phase (1962-9) *The Saint*, as everyone knows, drove a Volvo P1800. The Volvo was actually the

her car. Unfortunately, his wife saw him climbing in, and for the next two hours drove wildly over the roughest ▶

second choice car because the series producers had originally envisaged the hero in an E type Jaguar, but the Einsteins at Coventry, sharp as mustard when it came to free worldwide publicity opportunities, had turned them down. Hence when Ian Ogilvy took over in *The Return of the Saint*, a white XJS was dropped off by return of post. In the 1960s, though, Templar made do with his very striking Volvo, but if it had been me playing the Saint, I'd have used the bus.

'Sorry girls, no more room on top'.
Roger *sans* gloves.

The thing is, I once drove a P1800 and am still in therapy as a result. I remember it being like trying to control a rabid dray horse with reins made from dental floss. The steering was connected to something or other, but nothing that had any influence on the wheels and I can honestly say I have made better straight line progress on foot after a stag night. No way could this car have tackled a chase of any sort, which of course it didn't have to, because there was no budget for burning rubber.

The exception which proves the rule of my theory about good car/bad TV is *Randall And Hopkirk (Deceased)*, where one of the private detectives was a ghost (special effects budget: one white suit). This series managed to fit in both crap story lines AND crap cars, in this case a Mini and a Vauxhall Victor. *Randall And Hopkirk* was even worse than the American cop TV series *McCloud*, starring Dennis Weaver, and he drove a horse.

In truth, cars only got good on TV when the programme-makers stopped

country roads she could find outside their Italian village. A badly bruised and battered Stefano was eventually worrying about what they looked like and concentrated more on what they could do. For proof of this look no further than *The Sweeney*, the *Professionals* and *Starsky And Hutch*, the three greatest cop series ever, all of which featuring cars that squealed, rolled, crashed and burned. These programmes contained nothing you would find on a plinth at Goodwood being polished by a man in a Panama hat. Instead we had Capris, Granadas and Escorts: short on pose, long on purpose. Even Starsky's Gran Torino 460 V8 was relatively run of the mill.

The good telly cars also had one other thing in common: the blue oval badge on the radiator grille. Ford sussed quite early on the marketing potential of handing out cars to the TV companies, beginning in the 1960s by providing the Zephyrs for *Z Cars*. Admittedly, *Z Cars* action was hardly at *Terminator* levels, but things perked up considerably when Regan and Carter

Regan's Granada. Not Regan's snack.

loosened their ties for *The Sweeney*. All the car chase elements came together perfectly for this series about the London Flying Squad: the script-writers' typewriters were on steroids, there were plenty of cheap Mk2 Jags around for rolling and because the 1980s property boom was still some way off, there were acres of bombsites on which to unleash the rear-wheel-drive cops and robbers.

In the early episodes, Regan drove a manual Granada 3 litre S, but Mary Whitehouse's complaints about pick-axe handles and shooters meant the following series had to be toned down and made more realistic. Police consultants had also noted that Regan, as a Detective Inspector, would not be driving himself, so the 3 litre S was replaced by a Granada Ghia with

freed from the boot by Italian police. He is now divorcing his wife. ★BIZARRE★

'Blimey, Guv, how did you get back from that strip club last night?'

appropriately hefty driver. This left Regan free to complain about the food in the glove box: 'George, what's this pear doing here? I want ham, on white bread, in cellophane.'

It was Ford who also came to the rescue of the even more action-packed *Professionals*. At first the TV production company went for British Leyland vehicles and for a brief period Bodie, Doyle and Cowley drove a Triumph Dolomite, a TR7 and, if my memory serves me, a brown Austin Princess Vanden Plas; which was a truly staggering choice of vehicles for our front line crime-fighters. This was the 1970s, remember, when Leyland cars were so badly built they broke down before they got to to the end of the production line. TR7s in particular would collapse if you so much as shouted at them. But what caused the split between the TV *Professionals* and the Leyland amateurs was the incompetence of the car firm's publicity department, who insisted on taking their motors back off Bodie and Doyle in the middle of shooting so they could lend them out to local newspaper motoring correspondents. Quite understandably miffed at having to break off a major car chase to accommodate the *Glossop Chronicle*, the *Professionals* switched to 2.8 injection Capris and Escort RS 2000s.

Thus began a long and fruitful relationship, blighted by only one incident when a little old lady saw the *Professionals* crew loading some Kalashnikovs into the boot of a Capri. Not being *au fait* with prime time telly, she rushed home and phoned the anti terrorist squad... ★

HOW TO WRITE A TELEVISION DRAMA

L et's just say you've been charged with the task of writing a new television drama along the lines of *Morse*. Now, obviously, as with all TV programmes of this type, your central character is a twice-divorced maverick with a drinking problem that, with a great deal of effort, he's managing to control. He has four children but at weekends he is too busy flying model aeroplanes to see much of them. Of course, they hate him.

He is an accomplished piano player, suggesting he likes the finer things in life and yet he's never had a suit, and doesn't want one. He doesn't like estate agents and isn't that enamoured of his job. Inevitably, he and his immediate boss enjoy a love-hate relationship, made more difficult by the boss being married to one of our hero's ex-wives. Here's your problem. How, pray, do you get all that across, along with a plot line, within the first five minutes of your opening programme? Come on.

After chasing crooks in a Granada, John Thaw sees sense.

Come on. Time's money here. People are turning over. We're losing advertising revenue. HURRY UP. Well happily, it's all very simple. You just have him drive into the opening shot in a 1969 Mercedes 230SL. The car will tell us that he has an appreciation for the classics, and thus we'll understand he plays the piano. And because the SL was made with such loving attention to detail, we'll have him clocked instantly as the maker of model aeroplanes. Now this is an old car, of course, which tells us that he's a maverick. A non-maverick would have a standard-issue Police Vectra. And we know, too, from the convertible nature of this car that our man likes the wind in his hair. This means he's not that bothered about his appearance and *that's* why he never wears a suit. See? It's easy. You just show us the car and from that moment you can hit us with the plot.

This happens time and time again in modern television drama. Bergerac had that stupid old Triumph, letting us know straight away that here we have a Maverick cop who's not in a hurry. Spender had a Sierra Cosworth letting us know that he's a maverick cop who *is* in a hurry. Then there's *Morse*. Over the years, we've learned he likes a drop of real beer with twigs in it, crosswords, Mozart and that he has a classical education. Well of course he does. The man drives a Mark II Jag.

I remember a pilot show that for reasons I'll never understand never made it to full production (nor did its title stick in my mind). It featured the simply glorious Imogen Stubbs parading around in a pair of stockings that fell way short of her flouncy A-line mini-skirt. She was a dizzy private detective and, like all dizzy PIs, she had a Sunbeam Alpine. *Lovejoy* had a Morris 1000 with Wolfrace wheels... like he would. Kinsey had a sinister looking Merc with up and over headlamps. To match his mac. And Quentin Willson has a Daimler Dart.

When I'm old and gnarled, I'm going to write a television police series about a maverick cop with a drugs problem and two ex-wives. He'll have an angry boss, of course, and, naturally, a ruthless determination to succeed. Indeed, his determination to succeed will be so great that he'll still be doing the job even though, just a few weeks earlier, he won £22 million on a double roll over Lottery jackpot. This means he will have a Jaguar XJ220 and will have bought his sidekick, a weedy man who used to be a racing driver, a McLaren F1. It'll be the easiest show in the world to write because I won't need a plot at all. I'll just film them racing to work each week and half the world will tune in. You don't believe me? Well, each week on *Top Gear*, there's no story line, no character development and no twist in the tail. We just drive around in noisy, expensive cars and worldwide, we get 90 million viewers a week. The producer makes so much money he has a yacht in the Bahamas and a beach house in St Tropez.

(For libel reasons, I should explain that, in fact, the producer has a D registered Peugeot 205 and a rented flat in Birmingham. But I've always had a motto: never let the truth get in the way of a good story.) ★

★**BIZARRE** *17. Frederick Briener, a German schoolteacher, wrote to the police accusing his wife of ignoring road*

Reliant used to make Princess Anne's favourite car...

JOKE CARS

O f course, if you are engaged in the business of situation comedy, life is really very easy indeed. Del-Boy Trotter only needed to lumber into frame in his Reliant Robin van and the audience would start to convulse. If smoke were pouring from its exhaust, the seizures would start. And if it backfired, they'd die laughing. Then there's Mr Bean's Mini. Oh yes, how very funny. A Mini. Ha ha and indeed ha. But there is one car out there which gets an audience to die the instant they see it. I'm talking, of course, about the Morris 1000.

In fact, TV producers cannot realistically expect an audience to survive a comedy moment with the Morris 1000, which is why they resort to canned laughter. If a real live pensioner were to see Nurse Gladys Emmanuel showing her bloomers while climbing into the Morris during *Open All Hours*, you'd have a studio full of real dead pensioners. And it's much the same story with Frank Spencer. He can fall through the ceiling while

signs and traffic lights and of obtaining her licence by false pretences. Briener admitted that he was terrified of ▶

attempting to redecorate the loft and there'll be titters all round. But when he heads off to town to buy some supplies in a Morry Thou, well you're into a moment of comedy genius.

It's hard, really, to explain why this should be so. The Morris had a distinctly unfunny A series one litre engine which was capable of getting it from 0 to 60, and it wasn't desperately amusing through the corners, either. I think it may have something to do with the shape. A car with curvy wheel arches and a sloping boot has that cuddly feel. You don't want to drive it so much as tow it round the supermarket by one leg. At night, you want to dribble on it.

Give a car curves and it stops being a car. I dare say that in France, sitcoms rely on the Citroën 2CV and in Italy everyone falls about laughing whenever they see someone in a Fiat 500. But be assured that, in Germany, there is nothing funny whatsoever about ze VW Beetle. In fact, there is nothing funny about anyzing. I think, though, that the best use of a Morris 1000 came in Mike Leigh's classic TV play *Nuts In May*. It was used simply to define the character. Keith, the bearded enviro warrior with his hideous wife, Candice-Marie, enjoyed camping holidays, vegetarianism and folk music. He had to have a Morris 1000 but that wasn't the joke. It was merely a part of the puzzle that made the joke. ★

Frank Spencer in a moment of comedy genius.

MY TOP 20 DRIVES

THE CAR	Jaguar XJ220.
THE PLACE	Sennybridge, Wales.
THE DRIVER . . .	Me.
THE MEMORY . .	Putting my foot down for the first time. That car doesn't accelerate. It explodes.

his wife's driving, but he was even more terrified of his wife, and since she weighed 18 stones and he was only a

'Quentin, I'm sorry, but it really has had a charisma bypass.'

THE LEXUS PHENOMENON

t's an odd car, the Lexus. For years, the luxury car market has been dominated by Jaguar, Mercedes, BMW and Cadillac. They had good names and in the main made good cars. Toyota, however, felt it could do with a slice of the high profit margin action and started work on a car that would challenge the established stars. Obviously, they couldn't actually call it a Toyota because the name has no class. They knew that. They knew that Cabbage would have been better. Or Dog Turd, even. So the dreamed up the Lexus brand and introduced the LS400 – a car

ere ten, there was nothing else he could do. The courts found his wife innocent of the charges, fined Briener ▶

which did absolutely everything perfectly. It was the consummate all-rounder, able to cruise more quietly than a Rolls Royce, handle with the aplomb of a BMW and glide with the ease of a Jag. I'm sure Gary Lineker sees a little of himself in the Lexus, which is probably why he has one.

But Peter Gabriel – why on earth does the wackiest rocker of them all drive the least wackiest car ever to see the light of day? Well, Gabriel, remember, was sent to Charterhouse from where, I'm sure, he was expected to emerge with a raft of A-levels and a burning desire to be an accountant. Sure, he went off and did the rock star bit but now, as summer turns to autumn, our man is simply reverting to type. And the same goes for Bob Mortimer. Those suits do not sit terribly well with the Pleblon interior of a Lexus but, remember, before he teamed up with Vic Reeves, our man was a solicitor. 'Nuff said. The Lexus, you see, is the perfect middle England, middle class, middle of the road golfers car. It may be efficient but it has no soul. You climb in and after a little while you climb out to find you are somewhere else. It is as effortless and as interesting as being beamed around the countryside by Scottie. I'm told that Mike Baldwin has a Lexus and I'd love to be able to say what this means. But I have never, in my entire life, seen *Coronation Street*. So I can't.

I can conclude with this little sentiment, though. On *Top Gear*, Tiff with his boyish good looks and racing driver attitude has a 5 series BMW. I, as you know, run a super-charged Jaguar XJR. Which only leaves Quentin Willson. Here is a man who cares not one jot about a car so long as it never breaks down and depreciates horizontally.

Obviously, Quentin drives a Lexus. ★

MY TOP 20 DRIVES

THE CAR	Land Rover Discovery.
THE PLACE	Wave Hill Station, Australia.
THE DRIVER	Me.
THE MEMORY	I am an 18-hour drive from the nearest evidence of man's existence. It is 135 degrees out there. If this bloody thing breaks down...

THE GREATEST TV CAR OF THEM ALL

Steed's bulging Jag coupe. Emma Peel's Elan. Simon Templar's XJS. Lord Brett Sinclair's Aston and Jason King's Jensen. Over the years there have been a great many glorious cars in television drama but given the choice of owing just one, I'd go for Danny Wilde's Ferrari Dino 246GT. And already, I've made a mistake. You see, the red-blooded star of *The Persuaders* was not a Ferrari at all. You can poke about under the skin until the owner comes back and hits you with a large stick, but you won't find a single prancing horse. This car wasn't ever called a Ferrari. It was always simply the Dino... and no one knows why.

Sure, the 2.4 litre V6 engine was made largely by Fiat, the car itself was built by Scaglietti, a Torinese coachbuilders, and it was a Pininfarina design. So you might argue that it wasn't a Ferrari because Ferrari had nothing to do with it. But it was designed by Ferrari and the lower half of the engine was made in Maranello. You may argue that, at this time, a

Moore got the suits, Tony Curtis got the Dino. And the driving gloves.

Ferrari with a mere V6 under the beautiful bonnet didn't really count, but over the years Enzo had put his name to all sorts of race cars with V8s, V6s and even in line fours.

Some say Enzo would not allow the Dino to wear a prancing horse badge because its engine was also used by Fiat in their own Dino and by Lancia in the all conquering Stratos. But people can guess until the cows come home. The fact is that Enzo never told *anyone*.

I like to think the reason is very simple. If my son were killed and I was a motor industry mogul, I would name a car after him. And that would be the only name the car would ever have. Well Enzo's son, who was killed in 1957, was called Dino... And the car that bears his name is stunning – just like the man himself; it really is a baby Ferrari.

Though the 2.4 litre engine only produced 175 bhp putting it on level terms with, say, a Golf VR6, it was more than enough for the lightweight Dino. To get from 0 to 60 took just 7 seconds and the top speed was 147 mph. If you were deaf. And small. To get into that tiny cabin, where you find an instrument binnacle that's seemingly been lifted straight from the Daytona, you must have legs and arms which telescope like a car's aerial... and a head which can disappear into your shoulders. This was a car purpose built for Clive Anderson.

I drove one once and was deeply uncomfortable until I got past 3,000 rpm. Until then, not much happens but afterwards, with the chains

'Sod this. If he gets the Dino and the gloves, I'm off to be James Bond.'

thrashing away inches behind your head, it becomes louder than a hovering Harrier. The deep discomfort became ear-bleeding, head-splitting pain. I forgave it everything though in the first series of bends, which it scythed through with absolutely no fuss at all. Despite those old-fashioned tall tyres, this is utterly and completely perfect. You could put it on wheels made from margarine and wood, and it would still out-corner just about everything on the road. And out-pose them as well. The basic shape with those flying rear buttresses lives even today in the 355, but back then it was a revelation. Perfect proportions, perfect balance and a price that wasn't far short of perfect, either.

This, however, was very nearly the Dino's downfall. Because it was priced to compete with lesser cars, it was bought by people seeking primarily to enhance their image – people who didn't understand the first thing about supercars. They'd become used to not looking after their Mercs and Jags very well and felt that because the Dino was a quasi-Fiat, it too could handle the rough and tumble of everyday life. But it couldn't and over the years many were virtually destroyed by careless, abusive owners.

Happily, the boom times of 1989/1990 meant values soared and money was available to restore those early tatty Dinos into useable, even concours-winning classics. Today, you can buy a restored Dino for £50,000, leaving enough money to buy a bad jacket, team up with a Lord and save people from baddies. ★

THE REAL GIRL POWER STORY

In the beginning, men were barrel-chested and had clubs. Women wore furry bikinis and had children. For thousands of years, men were hunters, searching in the early days for food and, in more recent times, for the money to buy food. And women were the home-makers. However, in the last 30 years, women have decided they want to raise children, make the home *and* kill pigs. It's been a time of dizzying progress with women now flying fast jets, driving space shuttles, running countries and fronting rock bands. Turn on the television and you'll find pretty well every drama these days depicts women as strong, independent types and men as useless layabouts with nothing in their underpants – all of which, I guess, is fine. However, the womanisation of cars is only just beginning, and there are some worrying teething problems.

Here's the deal. Before a boy is out of nappies, he will be interested in cars, tractors and fire engines, and a girl won't. Ever since the internal combustion engine it has always been thus. Little girls like Barbie dolls.

★BIZARRE *18. When Belgian housewife Avril Gross got into her car to go shopping she was furious to find her*

Little boys like Bee Ems. Oh sure, there has always been the odd girl who's able to spot a Napier at a thousand paces but, by and large, cars are a man thing.

Until, that is, Mazda came along with the MX5. Never mind that it was a perfectly-balanced, front-engined, rear-wheel-drive sports car and never mind also that it handled like a rabbit, this car is so, so feminine it should really have been supplied with wings. It should have been on sale at the make-up department in Boots. And it's easy to see why.

(Left) Diana Rigg waits for the AA. (Above) Tara Palmer Tomkinson and an imitation Elan, the MX5.

First of all, it was never a desperately fast car, which meant it was never a serious threat at the lights. The shape, too, was more cat than leopard. It wasn't even slightly aggressive and, as such, was more suitable for the home-maker than the warmongering hunter-killer.

Women flocked to buy the MX5 and a whole new world opened before their very eyes. Here was a car that put some wind in your hair and bees in your teeth. It looked lovely and drove like a dream – the kind of dream where you win some money and can fly. Such was the success of this little car that pretty well every other designer in the world scurried off to his drawing board to come up with a rival.

Rover were one of the first out of the blocks with the MGF, a funky-looking mid-engined sports car which, in VVC form with the more powerful engine, is something of a road rocket. I'm sure they were expecting racing drivers all over the world to buy one, but instead they got Anthea Turner. And Emma Noble. Women were now driving sports cars that could shift.

And what about the supercharged Mercedes SLK, one of which is driven by Channel 5 presenter Julia Bradbury? She admits she has no clue about what happens under the bonnet and doesn't know what a supercharger is or does, but likes the SLK because it depreciates slowly. Wise girl: 'Men are the higher earners and have always been able to afford the TVRs, the

neighbour's car parked so close it made it impossible to get her own vehicle out into the traffic. After hooting her ▶

Julia Bradbury watches her SLK corner rapidly and depreciate slowly.

Ferraris and the Porsches,' she says, 'but the MX5 lowered the game standard so that women too, can now join in.'

And join in they have. The days when sports cars were driven exclusively by RAF officers who had black labradors are over. Car manufacturers say that, in 1997, roughly 15 per cent of sports cars were bought by women, but add that the figure does not account for husbands, buying a car for their wives or daughters, or companies buying for female staff. The figure could, and almost certainly is, much, much higher.

In the not too distant past, Katy Hill from Blue Peter would have been at home now with an ironing board and a second-hand Ford Fiesta. But instead, she's out driving her Porsche Boxster – a car she absolutely adores. Then there's Dani Behr, who likes to take on men at the lights in her BMW 328i. 'I let them get a little bit ahead then I floor it and say: "See ya",' she says.

And this, really, is the problem. Now that women are starting to drive round in nice cars, they are on level terms with men on the road and are waging a war they haven't bothered to declare. For years, men have trampled on women, refusing to let them work, vote or go out at night. And now women are fighting back by ensuring we're second away from the lights. My wife declared the other day that she would never again drive a car with less than 200 brake horsepower, and I strongly suggest that if you come alongside her at the lights in her BMW Z1 – *which doesn't actually fit the bill but don't tell her that* – you back off. As far as she's concerned, a traffic light grand prix is a race to the death.

And so it goes with *Sunday Times* columnist Tara Palmer Tomkinson. The blue-blooded embodiment of It-ness has a Honda NSX which has two speeds. Flat out, and just slightly more than flat out. TPT, as she's known in the trade, says she was brought up on a farm and knows all about cars. Right, Tara, so where's the engine in this thing? 'It's under my arse.' Nearly

horn fruitlessly for several minutes, she rang her neighbour's door bell and asked her to move her car. The

Clarkson corners Julia's SLK rapidly, while appreciating it slowly.

right. More worrying still, she didn't know that the NSX has a little button on the dash which, when pressed, turns the traction control off. I only hope she never uses it, because they'd hear about the resultant accident in Peru.

Tara drives like a man possessed. Every corner is taken on the very limits of adhesion and every traffic light is an excuse to break the clutch. When she wins, and she always, always does, the beaten driver gets the finger. Traffic jams are dealt with by going down the wrong side of the road and the rules of the road are treated as nothing more than guidance.

All the women I have talked to say they are regularly carved up and intimidated by men drivers, but I just cannot accept this. Sure, men carve people up but we don't do it specifically to women. We do it to everyone. When I dive in front of another man, causing him to brake or swerve, or preferably both, he doesn't burst into tears. He may do nothing, he may shake his fist or he may, in a bout of road rage, attempt to get past again, but at no point does he see it as a personal attack.

When a woman is carved up, though, she believes it is because she is a woman. And fights back on behalf of the sisterhood. Well now, listen girls, if you want equality, that's fine by me and I guess it's fine too by all right thinking blokes. But please accept that when you're on the roads, you're a person, not an underdog with a point to prove. ★

neighbour, Corinne Flavier, said she was busy washing her hair and would come out when she was finished. An ▶

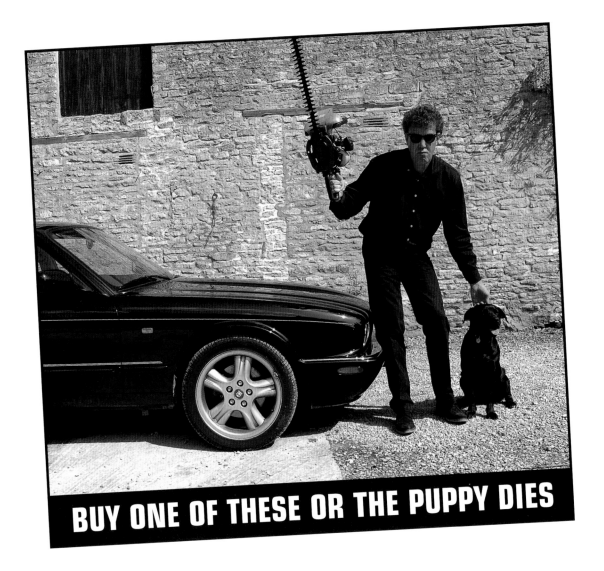

BUY ONE OF THESE OR THE PUPPY DIES

AN HONEST & VERY PERSUASIVE CAR AD

enraged Avril rushed back to her car and began nudging aside her neighbour's vehicle. Ms Flavier, head swathed in

SELLING CARS

Throughout the late 1980s and early 1990s, VW ran a series of commercials designed to show that their cars were well made. 'If only everything in life were as reliable as a Volkswagen,' went the strap-line. But two were never screened. The first, which could only be shown once a year, began with what appeared to be a white screen but was in fact a white desert stretching away to a white sky. After 15 seconds, an eternity in TV advertising, a tow truck lumbered into frame towing a Golf. It crossed the screen in the middle distance and was gone. And then, after another five seconds, a caption appeared: 'April Fool'.

The second was made for the 50th birthday of VW's advertising guru, Johnny Mezarus... *It's a night-time woodland scene and we see an owl hooting. The camera cranes down and, in a clearing, we find a Golf. The*

towels, rushed out, jumped in her car and drove it into Avril's. The women then began ramming each other until a ▶

registration plate is JM50 – it was Johnny Mezarus' 50th, remember. The windows are steamed up, the car is rocking gently from side to side and we hear, from inside, the excited squeals of a woman... and then it all stops. The car is still, and there is silence until we hear the woman say 'Don't worry Johnny, it can happen to anyone, especially when they're 50.' And we then see the closing caption: 'If only everything in life were as reliable as a Volkswagen.'

THE MOST EXPENSIVE TV CAMPAIGN

It can be good fun to divide the cost of a car commercial by the sales figures of the car it's trying to promote. It usually works out at a few hundred pounds per car, which is scary enough, but just once, it went off the scale. To launch Isuzu in Britain, the importers felt television advertising was an absolute must. Pizza Express would disagree, but there you are. So, they employed a top flight agency and a commercial was shot and screened for the new Piazza coupe.

Well, I've done the sums and it seems the cost of the campaign worked out at £8,000 per car. The importers, in case you're interested, went bust.

TOP 10 RUBBISH ADVERTISING STRAP LINES

1 'The drive of your life.' – What? The Peugeot 309 diesel?

2 'If only everything in life were as reliable as a VW.' – My Scirocco went through clutch cables like it was under medical orders to eat three a day.

3 'The ultimate driving machine.' I see, and the McLaren Mercedes isn't.

4 'Relax – it's a Rover.' No it isn't. It's a tarted up, overpriced Honda.

5 'Vorsprung Durch Technik.' Hitler used to say this, didn't he?

6 'First man, then machine.' Very nice, but what does this actually mean?

7 'Everything we do is driven by you.' Actually, everything they do is driven by a need to keep the shareholders happy.

8 'Nothing moves you like a Citroën.' So, apparently, we get more whipped up by a Xsara diesel than by Michelle Pfeiffer.

9 'Volvo. A car you can believe in.' No, I'm sorry, I don't believe in it. I don't believe there is any such thing as a Volvo.

10 'There's more to life with Renault.' Just change 'with' to 'than' and this would be about right.

crowd gathered. By the time the police arrived both cars were completely wrecked. ★BIZARRE★

THE WORST ADVERT OF ALL TIME

Honda got Martin Clunes to direct a commercial for the CRV sport utility car in which he and Neil Morrissey would star. It was hilarious. They were on the beach and turned off the public shower so that this pretty young girl would have to use the facilities in their Honda. And then – I can hardly write this down for laughing – a big ugly bloke turned up and wanted to use it as well. All it was missing was a speeded up section featuring Brian Rix and some polkadot boxer shorts.

But this pales into insignificance alongside Vauxhall's launchtime efforts with the Godawful Vectra. Realising that to show the whole car would invite people to stay away from the showroom in droves, they chose instead to film tiny bits of it, using a lens that seemed to have been dipped in marmalade. We were told nothing about the car, except that it had been designed for the next millennium. Well, in that case, would it be possible to bring the millennium forward a couple of years?

I was particularly annoyed by the advertisement for the people carrier in which the husband kept asking if he could drive. And his wife kept saying no. Speaking of husband and wife double acts, who can forget Nissan's Mr Jones, who drives to work even though he works at home? I work at home and I have a Ferrari in the garage but you can be assured that I don't drive to the office. I saunter. Then there's Peugeot's raunchy 306 commercial where Mrs Improbable gets so turned on by her husband washing the car, she had to have him on the kitchen table, immediately. Of course she did. Happens to me all the time. But the Most Excruciating Car Commercial Of All Time Award goes to... drum roll... Renault. And not to bloody Papa and Nicole, either. Sure, they both deserve a crisp backhand to the mouth but for sheer, toe-curling awfulness, they are beaten into second place by that git with his talking Megane, the 'car that speaks your language'.

In my house, we actively boycott products which are the subject of poor television campaigns. Which is why there is no Canon appliance in Telly Towers. Nokia phones are right out, too. And now we have vowed, in a solemn midnight ceremony involving blood and goats, that we will never buy, test drive or even talk about a Megane until the day we die. Not even the Scenic version which, irritatingly, is very good.

MY TOP 20 DRIVES

THE CAR	Dodge Viper.
THE PLACE	Putney Bridge, London SW6.
THE DRIVER . . .	Me.
THE MEMORY . .	Ten minutes earlier I had just said 'I do' at a church in Fulham and now I'm on my way with my new bride on a lovely sunny day, in a Dodge Viper, to a bloody great piss-up in Putney. And then we're going to the Virgin Islands. To a hotel called Little Dix, incidentally.

★BIZARRE *19. Spurned lover Charles Bryant decided to take revenge on his girlfriend*

BEST ADVERT OF ALL TIME

Obviously, car advertising exists primarily to sell cars, but at the same time it can be used to shape or change a car's image. And in the whole history of advertising I know of no campaign which did that quite so successfully as Volvo's recent televisual bombardment.

For sure, the new 850 was an infinitely nicer car to drive than its predecessors. From day one, the engineers and designers set out to make a car which encompassed all of Volvo's traditional values – porridge, soup and labradors. But in addition, they'd fitted whizzy suspension and a new and zestful engine which, in the top T5 model, was turbocharged. In other words, there were a whole new set of values – chilli, punk and Castrol R.

You see, advertising will only work if the product backs up the message. Vauxhall, for instance, told us that 'quality is a right, not a privilege', which is a good idea and will work right up to the moment when the Vauxhall you buy splutters to a halt one wet Friday night in November. So Volvo's ad men at Abbot Mead Vickers felt they could shout about performance, safe in the knowledge that people who bought the car would not be disappointed. They could even go to a British Touring Car race and see a Volvo just like theirs sweep aside the BMWs and the Alfas. They'd got a Volvo... which was sporty. Wow.

when he found her in bed with another woman. Car dealer Bryant stole back the Rolls Royce he had given his ▶

MY TOP 20 DRIVES

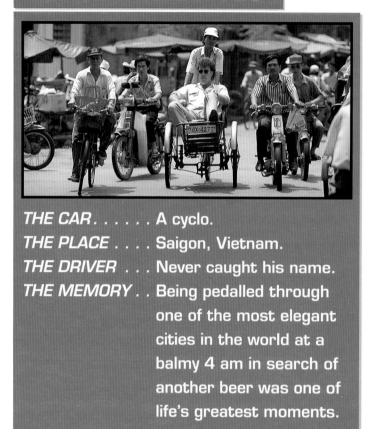

THE CAR . . . . . A cyclo.
THE PLACE . . . . Saigon, Vietnam.
THE DRIVER . . . Never caught his name.
THE MEMORY . . Being pedalled through one of the most elegant cities in the world at a balmy 4 am in search of another beer was one of life's greatest moments.

However, and this was the tricky bit, they didn't want to lose the old values completely. So we had a stuntman driving over the Corinth canal on railway tracks. We had a photographer driving down a runway, chasing a plane and we had Twister, where mad scientists drove into the heart of a tornado. Throughout the assault the message was clear: yes, this was a fast car which handled well, but it was strong and dependable, too. It was risk with complete control.

I think the best of the three, however, was Twister, an advert shot with no computerised, post-production trickery. It was filmed in California, mostly on the Edwardes Air Force base, where tornadoes are few and far between. So to create the wind effect, a helicopter blade was set in motion eight feet off the ground. Four cars were used and unusually for a car commercial, none was ever washed.

Then there was the house we saw explode as the tornado ripped it

girlfriend as a present and left in its place a one ton block of scrap metal with her number plate perched on top. An

apart. They did actually blow up a house, but the first time round it happened too soon when a short circuit set off the explosion before the cameras were ready. So they bought another house which imploded, and another, and another. Five houses were eventually destroyed before director Tony Kaye was happy.

And was Volvo happy? Well they spent an estimated half a million pounds on the commercial itself, plus another half million on *photographer* and another half million on *stuntman*, where they did actually build a bridge over the Corinth canal – a bridge that was shipped out from England and turned out to be too short. Then the Greek authorities wanted them to build it elsewhere. And there was only one crane in Greece capable of lifting the structure... which was in Athens, a four hour drive away.

Well it's four hours in a car but the crane could only do 5 mph, and the driver was in no hurry because he had the production company by the short penis hairs. So they paid him a fortune and they waited, and waited and waited. Then they had to pay for the screenings which cost them not several £ million per ad. So, the whole campaign cost God knows how many £ million and they sold loads and loads of 850s. Total cost per car: worth it. Improvement in brand awareness and respect? Total.

The best car advert ever then? Well it was damn sight better than most of the programmes that surrounded it, that's for sure.

RUNNER-UP

Renault – 'They've got Michael.' At the height of Renault's campaign where drivers of the charismatic little '5' were asked 'What's Yours Called?', some bright spark in London decided to start putting illegally parked cars in Prisoner Of War camps called pounds. Renault were quick to respond with a man rushing home to tell his wife, breathlessly, 'They've got Michael.' She wanted to know what 'They' wanted, to which he said angrily: 'What do they always want? Money.' And, of course, it turned out that Michael was their Renault 5, which had been towed away.

Today, of course, in Blair's Britain, the ad couldn't be screened because if Michael had been towed away, it must have been parked illegally. And parking illegally as we all know is now a crime to rival rape, murder and even genocide. ⭐

unrepentant Bryant said: 'I had to get my own back. The woman she was in bed with was my ex-wife.' ⭐BIZARRE

153

THE DECLINE OF ROLLS ROYCE

So, Rolls Royce is owned by the Hun and in the car industry world league, Britain, once in the top five, now comes just below Cameroon. British Leyland going down the toilet I can understand – it was hard for the workers to build quality cars when they were in the pub selling all the components, and you couldn't expect them to be in two places at once, but Rolls Royce? How the hell did we lose that?

At one time, every Royal, every film star and every shipping billionaire on the planet had a Crewe car. Even Lenin, not exactly a regular at Ascot, owned Rolls Royces. Back in the 1930s, an owner in Nepal wanted a Rolls so badly that he had it carried across mountain passes and gorges by 200 porters. But in recent years sales have dropped to the point where the company would have had to take in washing to fund future development.

★BIZARRE *20. The thickest insurance swindler in the world must be Frenchman Pierre Conte who, unable to keep*

The rumours about Gerry Anderson and Lady Penelope were unfounded.

Were the cars badly built? On the contrary, it's said you can place a fully-grown African elephant on a Rolls Royce and the car will give less than two inches. During his desert campaigns, Lawrence of Arabia did his fighting with a fleet of nine armoured Rolls Royces and in a typical day blew up several bridges, massacred a regiment of Turkish cavalry, destroyed railway lines and knocked out a couple of command posts. His chauffeur described the experience as a period of 'continuous hustle'.

Similarly, during the First World War the Duke of Westminster would patrol the front lines in his Rolls Royce to go Hun bashing. Later on, he fought in Egypt against the Senussi tribesmen. Backed up by four armoured Rolls Royces called Bulldog, Blast, Biter and Bloodhound, the Duke chased the fuzzy-wuzzies into the desert and blasted them into submission. So, if the cars are built like missile silos, maybe it's necessary for the owners. Well, now we're getting warmer, but you can count out the rich eccentrics: Rolls Royce has had lots of them as customers without suffering any resulting image problem. Take the Maharajas of India, for instance, who in the 1920s and '30s were reputed to be buying around a quarter of all Rolls Royce production.

up payments on his Porsche, decided to hide the car, fake a robbery claim, collect the insurance payout and drive ▶

The failed last-ditch attempt to hold off German buyers of Rolls Royce.

The Maharaja of Nandagoon customised his Rolls Royce, fitting a steering wheel made from elephant tusks. Vulgar? Not really, not by local standards. Another Maharaja then had his Rolls made out of silver, while yet another, when the Rolls Royce company annoyed him, had his six Silver Ghosts made into garbage trucks, as you would.

Closer to home, we had Field Marshal Sir Henry Wilson, who had a pathological loathing of London cabs and used to drive round in his Rolls Royce looking for taxis that he could force off the road. And the nemesis of Rolls Royce was not a lack of rich owners, on the contrary, things only started to go pear-shaped when there were too many. The problem began when showroom salesmen stopped greeting, as one customer was known:

his car again when the heat had died down. Unfortunately, Pierre's brainwave was to bury the car and then share

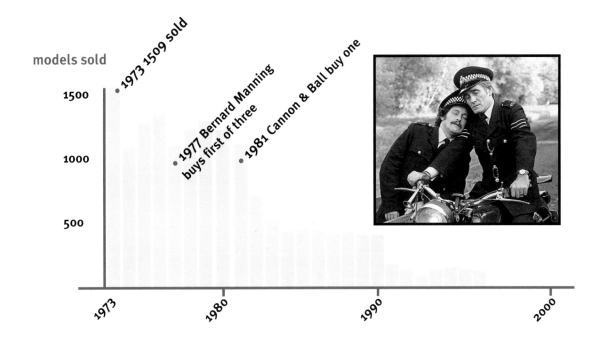

models sold

• **1973 1509 sold**

1500

• **1977 Bernard Manning buys first of three**

1000

• **1981 Cannon & Ball buy one**

500

1973   1980   1990   2000

'Lieutenant General His Highness Farzand-i-Khas-i-Daulat-i-Inglishia, Mansur-i-Zaman, Amirul-Umra, Maharaja Dhiraj Rajeshwar Shree, Maharaja-i-Rajgan, Maharaja Sir Bhupindra Singh, Mohinder Bahadur, Yadu Vanshavatans Bhatti Kul Bhushan, Maharaja Dhiraj of Patalia,' and instead started saying: 'Hello Tarby.'

Comics. That was the problem. They may deserve Queen's Awards to Industry for services to frilly dinner shirts, but they didn't half bugger up Rolls Royce. Look at the sales figures over the years and you'll note that John Lennon's psychedelic paint job doesn't have an effect on sales. Rolls Royce merely announced: 'It is not the company's policy to comment on owners' tastes,' and everything went on as normal. Likewise, Idi Amin on the log book was not a problem. But just look what happens when Cannon and Ball take delivery of a brace of Rollers. Freefall.

It's a sad fact but in the heart of the Home Counties Viscount Fotherington-Toff, who has probably heard very few jokes about ugly mothers-in-law, isn't really going to be interested in renewing his Rolls Royce when, over in Essex, cheeky chirpy cockney Mike Reid is screwing the number plate 'JOK IE' onto the front of his.

Today Rolls Royce could still be ours – if only, when the salesman saw Larry Grayson approaching, he'd shut that door. ★

his secret with a girlfriend he later dumped. The jilted lover went straight to the police, who dug up the car and ▶

'Curtis told me he'd left the gloves in here... urgh, is that emu dung?'

SOME CAR TV TRIVIA

★ **The Aston Martin belonging to Roger Moore's character Brett Sinclair in *The Persuaders* featured the number plate BS 1. The plate was borrowed from circus person Billy Smart.**

★ Terry from *Minder* is forever associated with his beat-up Capri, but he was originally given a Mk 2 Escort with flared arches. The *Minder* script-writers vetoed the car, saying he was too much of a loser to have a customised car, and went for a Capri instead. However, the Escort does appear in almost every episode of *Minder*: it's on Arthur's parking lot in the opening title sequence.

★ **Two 460 V8 Torinos were used in the making of *Starsky And Hutch*, but following the amazing success of the series, Ford produced 1002 Starsky Torino replicas for sale to the public. Even more amazingly, people actually bought them.**

found it rusting, with the interior destroyed by damp and the roof crushed in by the weight of the earth. Conte had

★ For the Pink Panther film *A Shot In The Dark*, car fanatic Peter Sellers had a Mini specially customised to include sunroof, leather interior and a tuned engine. The finished product cost almost as much as a Rolls Royce, with most of the cost going on the unique paintwork, which made the bodywork look like a wicker basket. Thousands of airbrushed lines had to be applied by a specialist customiser that Sellers knew. But before he could start the intricate work, the painter had to drink a bottle of whisky to relax his hands.

MY TOP 20 DRIVES

THE CAR. . . . . . A nitro injected V8 Jeep.
THE PLACE . . . . Iceland.
THE DRIVER . . . Ghisli Somethingorothersson.
THE MEMORY . . Last night my wife went into labour and now I'm climbing the vertical slope of a volcano... in a car. I want to be an accountant.

★ The Falcon V8 used by Mel Gibson in *Mad Max* is currently owned by dentist Peter Nelson at his Car's The Star Museum in Cumbria. Mr Nelson regularly receives requests to take the car on a tour of its native Australia, but has always refused. He fears – probably correctly – that once the Falcon gets back to its homeland, Australia's most notable contribution to the world of automation will be seized and impounded as a national treasure.

★ One of the greatest TV in-jokes ever occurs during the first episode of *The Dukes Of Hazzard*, when one of Bo and Luke's friends turns up in a red Ford Gran Torino with a white stripe. Yup, it was the same car used in *Starsky and Hutch*. ★

his car repossessed and was sent a £30,000 repair bill. ★ BIZARRE

PICTURE CREDITS

Advertising Archive 147
All Action 66, 73, 77, 81, 85, 118, 120, 143, 144
Alpha/Sport In General 105, 111, 124
Audi 94
BBC 135, 136
BMIHT 125
Neill Bruce . . .11. 21, 58, 61, 63, 71. 74, 82, 85, 92, 96, 100, 121, 139
Peter Roberts Collection/Neill Bruce 106, 114
Canal + Image UK 57, 132, 142, 154
Citroen 116
Eon Productions (via Ronald Grant Archive) 9
Ford 123, 125
Ronald Grant Archive 10, 12, 16, 18, 22, 23, 24, 29, 31, 32, 37
Ronald Grant Archive 39, 40, 48, 49, 50, 51, 85, 87, 157
Honda 149
Jaguar/Daimler Heritage Trust 76, 85, 125
London Transport 85
Mirror Syndication 98
Chris Moore 84
Moviestore Collection 14, 17, 33, 34, 36, 85, 103
Pictorial Press 41, 42, 43, 55, 56, 59, 62, 63, 64, 67, 68, 102,
Pictorial Press 110, 112, 128, 130, 140, 141, 155, 156
Rex Features 52, 69, 88, 89, 91, 93, 95, 101, 108, 113, 133
Rover Group 52
Toyota UK 19
Volvo UK 151
Andy Willman 72, 104, 152, 159

Planet Dagenham logo photo, models on page 6 and cover portrait
by Barry J Holmes for JMP Ltd.
All other Jeremy Clarkson photography by Roger Dixon for JMP Ltd.